GRANDSTANDING

GRANDSTANDING

The Use and Abuse of Moral Talk

Justin Tosi

Brandon Warmke

OXFORD
UNIVERSITY PRESS

OXFORD
UNIVERSITY PRESS

Oxford University Press is a department of the University of Oxford. It furthers
the University's objective of excellence in research, scholarship, and education
by publishing worldwide. Oxford is a registered trade mark of Oxford University
Press in the UK and certain other countries.

Published in the United States of America by Oxford University Press
198 Madison Avenue, New York, NY 10016, United States of America.

CIP data is on file at the Library of Congress
ISBN 978–0–19–090015–1

3 5 7 9 8 6 4

Printed by Sheridan Books, Inc., United States of America

For
David and Maria Tosi
and
Tom and Jann Warmke

TABLE OF CONTENTS

PREFACE

Many of us feel uneasy about the way people talk in public about morality and politics. We suspect that most people sense something is going wrong in these discussions. But beyond pointing to various cases of excessive shaming, rushes to judgment, and other bad behavior, it's hard to describe exactly what the problem is.

This book offers a diagnosis for a significant cause of bad behavior in public moral discourse. Much of our discourse is so awful because it consists of moral grandstanding—roughly, the use of moral talk for self-promotion. Don't get us wrong. We think moral talk is a good thing. People need to be able to talk about justice, freedom, equality, and the right thing to do. But we need to do so in ways that do good, and not just make ourselves look good. Grandstanders are too concerned with the latter.

Grandstanding is not associated with any particular political outlook. People with all sorts of views can and should come together to condemn grandstanding. It's not a partisan phenomenon. It's a human phenomenon. If you're honest with yourself, you can probably think of times when you were at least *tempted* to grandstand.

(We certainly can.) A once-enthusiastic participant in the online culture wars recently reflected on his history of grandstanding:

> Every time I would call someone racist or sexist, I would get a rush. That rush would then be reaffirmed and sustained by the stars, hearts, and thumbs-up that constitute the nickels and dimes of social media validation.[1]

This admission is both striking and bizarre. Why do we participate in such rituals? Why do we care whether our moral talk earns tokens of approval from people, many of whom we barely interact with? And why are we willing to throw people under the bus to get that approval?

This book is our attempt to make sense of grandstanding, and to tell you what we've learned about it over the past five years. Using evidence from the social and behavioral sciences, we'll explain why people grandstand and why it takes the forms it does. Using the tools of moral philosophy, we'll argue that grandstanding is a moral problem on all three major moral theories: it has bad consequences; it is a way of failing to treat people with respect; and it is not virtuous. Finally, using a bit of both science and philosophy, we'll talk about why grandstanding is a problem in politics, and what we can do to improve our moral discourse.

Some readers will have noticed that we mentioned the internet and social media. That theme runs throughout the book. But this is not a book about social media. It is a book about moral talk. Moral grandstanding is not a new phenomenon, and it did not begin with the rise of the internet. But for better or worse, most public discussion about morality and politics now takes place on the internet, where it is easier than ever to find an audience for your demonstrations of what a good person you are. If mentions of social media bore you, feel free to pretend that we're all still meeting in person at the Forum to see who despises Carthage the most, or the salon to see who is most committed to Enlightenment values. The psychology and behavior are the same. The medium makes some difference, but grandstanding has been with us for a long time, and you will recognize what we have to say about it even if you've never touched a computer.

But we do think that moral talk is different now that so much of it takes place online. Why? We don't have a tale to tell about new technology and the rapid decline of civilization, but our means of communication has likely had an impact on some features of our discussions. It is easier than ever to find an audience for your every thought, and to broadcast your message. Hundreds of millions have a platform to speak immediately to hundreds, thousands, or even millions of people. Because of this you also have more competition than ever for people's attention. To stand out, sometimes you have to do something special. As we'll discuss later, this has important effects on the content of our discussions.

It's also become easier to find and consume moral and po-litical discussion. That means we're probably exposed to more grandstanding now than ever before, even though there have al-ways been prolific grandstanders. In fact, instead of saying that grandstanding is easier to find than ever before, it might be more ac-curate to say that grandstanding is harder to avoid than ever before.

Finally, because it is now easier to find others' moral talk, it is also easier to monitor and harass people with whom you disagree. Those who discuss ideas for a living are the most acutely aware of this fact. Journalists are routinely pummeled with hateful messages for writing things people don't want to hear regarding their fa-vorite (or, alternatively, most despised) political figures. Academics who run afoul of the latest ideological trends in their fields are threatened with professional excommunication and worse. And occasionally even unsuspecting bystanders will wander into the minefield that is our contemporary culture war, and feel the wrath of an attention-seeking mob.

For some, it takes being on the receiving end of others' aggressive grandstanding to recognize—publicly, at least—that something is going wrong in public moral discourse. Our hope in writing this book is that you won't have to find out the hard way that grandstanding is a moral problem. This book can show you what's happening, explain why it's wrong, and give you some idea of what you should and shouldn't do about it.

Lubbock, Texas
Bowling Green, Ohio

ACKNOWLEDGMENTS

We began writing about this topic in the spring of 2014. Since then, we have had countless fruitful discussions with too many generous friends and colleagues to list here. We apologize to those we have omitted.

We received beneficial feedback on an early draft of chapter 4 in the spring of 2018 during a workshop on moral and political philosophy at the University of Michigan. We thank philosophers Jonny Anomaly, Dan Jacobson, Steven Wall, Philippe Lemoine, Spencer Jay Case, Hrishikesh Joshi, and Nevin Climenhaga for helping to improve that chapter.

In the summer of 2018, the Georgetown Institute for the Study of Markets and Ethics at the McDonough School of Business kindly held a manuscript workshop for an early draft of the book. We thank the Institute and Jason Brennan for inviting us, and participants Bryan Caplan, Michael Douma, William English, Robin Hanson, John Hasnas, Peter Jaworski, Loren Lomasky, and Thomas Mulligan for their comments on the book.

In the spring of 2019, the Institute for Humane Studies put together an interdisciplinary manuscript workshop on an advanced draft of the book. We thank both IHS and all the participants who read the entire book and gave us incredibly helpful feedback and advice over the course of two full days: Adam Arico, Paul Blaschko, Gabriel Brahm, Bill Glod, Bradley Jackson, Lee Jussim, Melanie Marlowe, J.P. Messina, Kathryn Norlock, Clay Routledge, Sean Stevens, Kyle Swan, and Fabian Wendt.

Several of Brandon's colleagues at Bowling Green State University have provided helpful feedback on several parts of the book. These included Christian Coons (who also coined the term "showcasing" from chapter 5), Molly Gardner, Max Hayward, and Kevin Vallier. Michael Weber gave especially detailed comments on the manuscript. We also are grateful for a generous group of Bowling Green philosophy graduate students who read the manuscript in a reading group in the fall of 2018 and offered extensive and helpful feedback: Joshua Brown, Christina Depowski, Ryan Fischbeck, Sara Ghaffari, Ezekeal Grounds, Mark Herman, Vassiliki Leontis, Amitabha Palmer, and Xuanpu Zhuang. Will Lugar gave us careful and detailed written comments on every chapter.

Over the years, Craig Warmke and Nathan Ballantyne have helped us solve lots of problems and given us wise advice and support. Several philosophers read and offered advice about individual chapters. For their time and good sense, we thank Howard Curzer, Brian Leiter, and Christian Miller. That we have received help from so many people does not mean that they endorse the contents of the book, of course. Furthermore, all errors are ours.

We presented portions of material at various places. We thank those institutions for inviting us and for the feedback we received: Northern Illinois University, Wake Forest University, the University of Michigan, the North Carolina Philosophical Society,

Creighton University, the Center for Democracy and Technology in Washington, D.C., and the Canadian Centre for Ethics and Public Affairs in Halifax, Nova Scotia.

Brandon met Josh Grubbs at new faculty orientation at BGSU in the fall of 2016. It didn't take much convincing for Josh to see grandstanding as a topic ripe for investigation using the tools of empirical psychology. He has now put up with us for three years and shepherded with great care the social scientific study of grandstanding into a maturing research program. We thank him for throwing himself into this project and for helpful consultation on several empirical questions.

Greg Jenkins at Madhouse Creative worked closely with us to design the cover art. We were fortunate to have two editors work on the book. Our freelance editor, Shane Maxwell Wilkins, read an early draft of the book and gave us detailed, incisive feedback on both the substance and the form of our prose. Our editor with Oxford University Press, Lucy Randall, has been understanding, patient, and supportive. Her wise comments on the penultimate draft made the book far better than it otherwise would have been.

Chapter 1

Moral Talk Is Not Magic

"HOW ABOUT YOU GET CANCER"

Children can be horrible to one another. They bully, ostracize, ridicule, tease, and name-call. Many kids feel the need to win no matter who gets hurt, and respond to any criticism with aggression. They blame others when bad things happen, and gang up on those who are different.[1]

Many of the most important lessons we learn growing up are about how to treat people better. For most people, these lessons are effective. By the time we reach adulthood, most of us have learned to respect and empathize with others. However, many adults also learn to be selective in applying these lessons. Twitter offers a never-ending supply of examples. In 2016, a two-year-old boy from Nebraska was killed by an alligator at a resort in Orlando, Florida. Tragic. Twitter user @femme_esq, had another take, however, announcing to her twelve thousand followers:

> I'm so finished with white men's entitlement lately that I'm really not sad about a 2 [year-old] being eaten by a gator [because] his daddy ignored signs.[2]

On October 1, 2017, a gunman opened fire on the crowd at a concert in Las Vegas. The shooter killed 58 and injured 851 others. Again, tragic. Yet a CBS legal executive tweeted a different take, connecting the Vegas shooting with the Sandy Hook school shooting which left 20 children dead:

> If they wouldn't do anything when children were murdered I have no hope that the Repugs will ever do the right thing. I'm actually not even sympathetic [because] country music fans often are republican gun toters.[3]

Starting in 2013, feminist media critic Anita Sarkeesian produced a series of videos criticizing the portrayal of women in video games. Her efforts were met with mountains of abusive tweets. A sample:

> How about you get cancer.

> Just putting it out there, you deserve all those death threats you are getting.

> "Harassing" will continue and accelerate. We're not going to stop until no one will openly admit to being feminist.

These were some of the tamer responses.[4] Many involved threats of sexual violence, incitement to suicide, and death threats.

We have no trouble recognizing that this sort of behavior is unacceptable from children. Imagine the horror you would feel upon discovering that your child told her friends she wasn't even sad about a recent bus accident, since the kids on board were from a rival elementary school. Or imagine learning that your child had threatened a classmate with sexual violence for criticizing his favorite video game.

But many adults act as if this kind of abusive behavior is perfectly acceptable when they discuss morality or politics. We don't allow our children to mock, shame, or gang up on others. But if *we* mock, shame, or gang up on people who express moral views that we find offensive, that's different. Or so these adults seem to believe. You don't need to spend much time perusing social media, watching cable news, or discussing politics in mixed partisan company to know that public discourse is one big, rowdy adult schoolyard.

Perhaps you think this comparison between adult public discourse and child misbehavior is naïve. Maybe you think it comes from a place of privileged ignorance. Sure, when people defend their moral beliefs and values, conversation can become heated. But that's because people care deeply about morality. And if you really care about what is right and wrong, then it shouldn't bother you that moral talk can be rough. If someone expresses moral views that offend you, it is fair game to tell them in no uncertain terms that they are despicable. That's just public moral discourse—the grown-ups are talking.

We think people who take this view of moral talk are unaware of the damage that moral talk can cause. Much moral talk is good. But some of it isn't. Let us explain.

MORAL TALK

By "moral talk" we mean communication about moral matters—topics like justice, human rights, and, more generally, who is morally good and what morally ought to be done. More specifically, moral talk might include any of the following:

- Talk about rights, dignity, justice, and respect: "Immigration is a fundamental human right," and "We need justice for Anton."

- Talk about whether someone did something morally right or wrong: "She did the right thing by calling out her accuser," and "He certainly harassed all those women."
- Talk about how morally good or bad someone is: "He was incredibly brave," and "She is dishonest."
- Talk about what should happen to people who do good or bad: "She deserves all our admiration," and "To hell with him."
- Talk about moral emotions: "I am outraged that she told those vile lies," and "I greatly admire him for the sacrifices he made for his family."
- Talk that recommends for or against social policies: "We have a duty to future generations to reduce carbon emissions," and "Justice demands that we practice capital punishment."

Such moral talk is extremely valuable. It is our primary means of bringing morality to bear on practical problems. We use it to warn of threats and identify people who do others harm. We publicly praise people who are worthy of trust. We spur positive social change with stirring speeches about our shared moral ideals. We influence the behavior of others simply by uttering phrases of moral condemnation. In short, moral talk is a powerful and important social tool for making ourselves, our neighbors, and our world better.

Since moral talk is so important, you might expect that it would be universally revered. At the very least, you would think that people would use the tools of moral talk carefully and responsibly, being sure not to deploy them for ill. That way, everyone would take moral talk seriously when it is needed. We would all know that when someone pulls out the big guns—appeals to rights, justice, dignity, respect, and so on—it is time to set petty concerns aside and have a serious discussion about important matters, unimpeded by trivia, ephemera, and personal squabbles.

Unfortunately, many people use moral talk irresponsibly. They use it to humiliate, intimidate, and threaten people they dislike, impress their friends, feel better about themselves, and make people less suspicious of their own misconduct. These are abuses of moral talk. The problem is not merely that people are being uncivil, but that they are co-opting moral talk for inappropriate purposes. When people use moral talk this way, they turn a protective instrument against the very people it is meant to help.

Treating moral talk as a free-for-all hurts other people, sometimes greatly, as we will explain throughout this book. Nasty moral talk is also destructive in another way. When it is common, people can become convinced that the whole practice of moral talk is not worth engaging in. To those who become so disaffected, moral talk comes to look like just a series of mean-spirited and implausible claims. So they opt out.

But apparently, many people don't see the downside of abusing moral talk. They act as if moral talk is always admirable (at least when their side does it). For these people, moral talk is magic. Invoking sacred words—justice, dignity, rights, equality, or honor, tradition, faith, family—magically transforms your nasty, abusive, selfish behavior into something heroic and praiseworthy. Want to be cruel to those people you don't like and have your like-minded peers congratulate you? Wrap your behavior in high-flying moral language. Voila! Brave, Admirable, Speaking Truth to Power.

But moral talk is not magic. We do not have free rein to treat others badly simply because we are invoking sacred words, or because we are showing in our own way that we care. Being morally outspoken is not itself an achievement. We are reminded of those who praise people for reading gossip magazines: "At least they're reading. Good for them!" Unlike most nasty moral talk, there may be nothing morally objectionable about this sort of reading. But it is surely not admirable. Just as adults shouldn't be credited for just any kind of reading, they shouldn't be credited for just any kind of moral talk. Not all moral talk is laudable, and the world would be better if some of it went away.

Moral talk has a job to do. It has a point: to help us become better people, treat others with the respect they deserve, and make our world a better place. But not every instance of moral talk helps us do these things. It's possible to abuse moral talk. And when we do, we can end up undermining our efforts at moral improvement.

Using moral talk well requires understanding how it can go wrong. Some ways of abusing moral talk are more or less obvious. Name-calling when you disagree with someone's lifestyle or moral views is typically frowned upon. Most recognize that it's wrong to tell someone she deserves to die because she committed a minor indiscretion. Some destructive forms of moral talk are subtler, though no less poisonous. This book is about one kind of poison to public discourse: moral grandstanding.

We will go into greater detail in the next chapter, but if you're looking for a "bumper-sticker" description, moral grandstanding is the use of moral talk for self-promotion. To grandstand is to turn your moral talk into a vanity project. Grandstanders are moral showboaters trying to impress others with their moral credentials. To get a better sense of what grandstanding is, let's look at some examples.

GRANDSTANDING: FROM HARVEY WEINSTEIN TO ROY MOORE

Most readers will have a general sense of what grandstanding is, if for no other reason than the frequency with which the term is invoked in contemporary politics. For instance, in 2013, then-President Obama criticized congressional Republicans for grandstanding as they threatened to shut down the federal government over a dispute about funding for the Affordable Care Act. "This grandstanding has real effects on real people," said Obama.[5] The L.A. Times editorial board also accused congressional Republicans of grandstanding over their efforts to defund Planned Parenthood.[6] The Brookings Institute called Mitt Romney's rhetoric on Iran in 2012 grandstanding.[7] Ross Douthat characterized then-candidate Donald Trump's pitch to his blue-collar supporters as no more than "the perpetual distraction of Twitter feuds and pseudo-patriotic grandstanding."[8] Trump's 2016 U.S. presidential campaign website included the line "We need real solutions to address real problems. Not grandstanding or political agendas."[9] And as President, Trump called former FBI Director James Comey a showboat and a grandstander while providing his rationale for firing him.[10] Trump said the same of John McCain over the latter's vote against the repeal of the Affordable Care Act.[11] You get the picture.

People throw around accusations of grandstanding fairly often. But what does grandstanding look like? Consider the example of Harvey Weinstein, the famous movie producer and Hollywood mogul. In the fall of 2017, dozens of women accused Weinstein of numerous acts of sexual harassment and assault. On October 5, Weinstein issued his first public statement addressing the allegations. He opened by noting that he "came of age in the 60s and 70s, when all the rules about behavior and workplaces were different." He then expressed remorse for his years of misbehavior and committed to doing better in the future, saying that he "so respect[s] all women and regret[s] what happened." But for our purposes, the interesting part of the statement comes at the very end:

I am going to need a place to channel [my] anger so I've decided that I'm going to give the NRA my full attention. I hope Wayne LaPierre [CEO of the National Rifle Association] will enjoy his retirement party . . . I'm making a movie about our President, perhaps we can make it a joint retirement party. One year ago, I began organizing a $5 million foundation to give scholarships to women directors at USC. While this might seem coincidental, it has been in the works for a year. It will be named after my mom and I won't disappoint her.[12]

Weinstein's remarks were universally panned. Observers of all political stripes could see that Weinstein was dangling his intention to further progressive political causes to distract from his misdeeds. He may have made mistakes, but he is a Good Person. He hates the NRA. He is duly critical of President Trump. Incidentally, he created a scholarship for women. We're pretty confident he was grandstanding.

Or consider another case. Also, in the fall of 2017, Alabama Republican Roy Moore ran against Democrat Doug Jones in a special election for US Senate. Moore has had a long, controversial career—including his own history of sexual misconduct allegations—the details of which we won't dig into here. What interests us is that he is often accused of grandstanding. Before the Alabama special election, Michelle Cottle of *The Atlantic* opined, "A pugilistic, self-aggrandizing grandstander like Moore is exactly what Alabama doesn't need representing its interests."[13] Doug Jones, Moore's opponent, described him as a grandstander as well. In one television campaign ad, Jones looked straight into the camera and told viewers that the health care system is "broken" and that "Roy Moore's extreme views and grandstanding will do nothing to fix it."[14] David French, writing for *National Review*, called Moore "a half-wit, grandstanding constitutional ignoramus."[15]

The accusations are not without merit. Immediately upon becoming chief justice of the Alabama Supreme Court, Moore ordered a 5,280-pound granite monument be inscribed with the Ten Commandments and placed in the Alabama judicial building. Several civil liberties groups sued, claiming the monument was unconstitutional. Moore lost the case and was ordered to remove the monument. He refused, and was ultimately removed from the bench for defying court orders. Throughout, he was adamant in defending the monument on moral and religious grounds. At one press conference, three months before his removal from office, Moore brought out the heavy moral artillery.

> As chief justice of the state of Alabama, it is my duty to administer [the] justice system of this state, not to destroy it. I have no intention of removing the monument of the Ten Commandments and the moral foundation of our law. To do so would, in effect, be a disestablishment of the justice system of this state. This, I cannot and will not do. But in a larger sense, ladies and gentlemen, the question is not whether I will remove the monument. It's not a question of whether I will disobey or obey a court order. The real question is whether or not I will deny the God that created us and endowed us with certain inalienable rights that among these are life, liberty and the pursuit of happiness.[16]

Perhaps this is the stand that God wanted Moore to take. An alternative explanation is that Moore wanted the people of Alabama to know that no power on earth, high or low, could move him from his moral conviction that a granite monument was crucial to the protection of our inalienable rights. What exactly is the connection between the monument and those rights? It's unclear. What does seem clear is that Moore wanted the voters of Alabama to think of him as a moral paragon, standing up for religion and the moral foundations of the law. Again, we're pretty confident he was grandstanding.

Although celebrities and politicians are perhaps especially liable to grandstand, they have by no means cornered the market. Your social media feeds are full of people trying to prove that they are on the right side of history. Thanks to them, public discourse has become a war of moral one-upmanship. You have probably seen people start out by discussing the merits of gun control only to end up trying to convince others that they care the most about elementary school children.

Many people are quick to agree that public discourse is in a sorry state, though often what they have in mind is the behavior of the "other side." It's easy to recognize bad behavior in other groups. It's harder to recognize it in our own group, let alone in ourselves.

This is a book about looking at ourselves squarely and honestly and asking whether we are *doing* good with our moral talk, or just trying to *look* good. We will show you that trying to look good with your moral talk is the very thing that prevents you from using it for good.

HOW TO CRITICIZE THIS BOOK

Because accusations of grandstanding have recently become another weapon in the culture wars, discussions about it tend to be heated and chaotic. We want to spur progress in this debate, not create drama. So, before we get into the details of moral grandstanding and why we think it's dangerous, let us clarify some things you may have started to worry about and give a short preview of what lies ahead.

As you will already know by now, moral talk can be abused. Although it promises to be about things we can all agree are important—justice, fairness, freedom, and the like—it can have negative effects when it goes wrong, like when we grandstand. In the next chapter, we'll explain exactly what moral grandstanding is, although you will have recognized it from the examples we've seen and those you encounter every day.

As we unpack moral grandstanding, you might understandably have some doubts. You may wonder: Are people ever really grandstanding? Or, even if people do grandstand, why think that it's common? If it's just a rare incident here and there, maybe it doesn't matter much.

Over the course of this book, we will try to persuade you that not only do people grandstand, many of us do it regularly. Of course, even if you agree that there is a lot of grandstanding going on, you still may think our own theory of moral grandstanding is mistaken. If that happens, we hope to hear from others about how to improve our understanding of what grandstanding is and how it works.

We also think that moral grandstanding is a way of abusing moral talk—that it is generally bad, and that we should avoid doing it. We give lots of arguments to try to convince you of this. Maybe you won't be convinced by all of them. But that's okay. As long as most of them are good arguments, we think we will have shown that grandstanding is generally bad and to be avoided.

There are some other objections that readers might raise that we'd like to try to address up front. Although we view them as non-starters, they might prevent readers from staying open to our views, so we want to discuss them briefly here. A critic might point out that grandstanding is not the worst or the most common way of abusing moral talk. But we don't claim either of these things, and our argument doesn't depend on them. Someone might object, however, that we shouldn't be writing a book addressing an abuse of moral talk unless it is the most serious or common form. But no one seriously believes the "discuss only the worst problem" principle. No one thinks that you shouldn't write a book on the problem of sexual harassment on college campuses because there are more serious transgressions on campus, such as sexual assault, or because some wrongs are more common, such as lying or plagiarism. And even if that principle were true, it would at best show that we were *morally* wrong to write this book rather than another one. It would not show that any of our arguments fail.

One final line of possible but unpromising criticism deserves special attention. Since our topic concerns the morality of public discourse, some will be drawn to the claim that our argument somehow conflicts with valuing free speech. The thought, we suspect, is that because we aim to show that some instances of public expression are morally suspect, then we must also think that people don't have a right to speak their conscience. But this is a mistake. Nothing in this book conflicts with a robust right to free speech. At the same time, having a right to say whatever you want does not mean that it is morally good to say whatever you want, and in whatever manner you want to say it. To see this point more clearly, think of lying. Everyone recognizes that in many circumstances it is morally wrong to lie. But no one thinks that you must choose between thinking lying is wrong and affirming a right to free speech.

In the next five chapters, we'll explain what grandstanding is, and give our reasons for thinking it is wrong. After we've laid out our argument, we will switch gears to look at how grandstanding affects politics in democracies, and then we will conclude the book by suggesting things that we can all do to improve the current state of moral talk.

So if you're the kind of person who cares deeply about justice, read on.

Chapter 2

What Is Moral Grandstanding?

GRANDSTANDING: A VERY SHORT INTRODUCTION

Not all grandstanding is of the moral variety. After all, there are all sorts of ways we can show off for others. The first recorded use of the term "grandstand" in the sense of "showing off" is from a book on American baseball published in 1888. The term was used to describe baseball players who liked to show off after making an impressive play: "It's the little things of this sort which makes [*sic*] 'the grand stand player.' They make impossible catches, and when they get the ball they roll all over the field."[1] The idea must have been that such players were playing to the cheap seats—to those in the grandstands.

Grandstanding also appears in other fields, as people engage in the relevant activities with an eye toward impressing others. Many of us have friends or colleagues who engage in intellectual grandstanding by taking advantage of conversations to display a sharp intellect or great depth of knowledge. You may also be familiar with what could be termed religious or spiritual grandstanding. After inviting your church deacon over to watch the Super Bowl, he announces to all within earshot that he's surprised you have time for that sort of thing, and that Sunday night is his allotted time to pray for all the missionaries, so regrettably, he won't be able to make it. In short, if there is a socially desirable quality that can be shown off through speech, someone has probably tried it.

The term "grandstanding" seems to have caught on more widely in the latter half of the twentieth century. A 1970 review of Noam Chomsky's book *At War with Asia* appearing in *The Harvard Crimson* includes the line "for those of us who aren't satisfied that we can end the war with a little Saturday afternoon grandstanding on Boston Common, doing something meaningful about terminating the conflict is still in the talking stage."[2] A 1975 piece in *The New Republic* accused the seventh U.S. President, Andrew Jackson, of engaging in "grandstanding defiance of the Supreme Court."[3] In 1976, Roger Ebert wrote in his review of Claude Chabrol's film *Just Before Nightfall* that "The movie's a meditation on guilt. When the husband determines to turn himself in, his wife accuses him of grandstanding. Both the wife and the friend very sincerely regret the murder, of course, but to involve the police . . . well, that would be going a bit far."[4]

We have now come to the point when the term is part of the universal lexicon that Americans use to discuss morality and politics. When you see a cable news host accuse Speaker of the House Paul Ryan or Senator Bernie Sanders of grandstanding, you have a rough idea what the accusation is. In this book, we clear up that picture and help you understand what it means to grandstand, specifically in moral contexts.

THE BASIC ACCOUNT OF MORAL GRANDSTANDING

As we've seen from these examples, the term "grandstanding" is used in many different areas of life. So what are *we* talking about when we talk about grandstanding?[5] Here is our basic account.

1. Grandstanders want to impress others with their moral qualities. We call this the **Recognition Desire**.
2. Grandstanders try to satisfy that desire by saying something in public moral discourse. We call this public display the **Grandstanding Expression**.

You can therefore think of grandstanding in terms of a simple formula:

Grandstanding = Recognition Desire + Grandstanding Expression

Let's discuss each of these two elements in some more detail.

The Recognition Desire

Grandstanders want others to think that they are morally impressive. This is the Recognition Desire. It is the first part of the Basic Account of grandstanding.

Just like you might try to look busy at work to get others to believe that you are hard-working, grandstanding is a means people use to make others think they are morally impressive. Sometimes, grandstanders want others to think that they are moral saints, or moral heroes. But other times a grandstander might have more modest aims. She might simply want others to think she is a morally decent person. In a world where precious few meet the threshold of moral respectability, she at least clears that bar. For instance, a grandstander might want others to recognize that although virtually no one cares enough about immigrants, she does. Whether she wants to be seen as morally great, or merely morally decent, she typically wants to be seen as better than someone or some group. It will be helpful to have a term to describe what the grandstander wants. Let's simply say that the grandstander wants to be seen as "morally respectable."

Sometimes the grandstander wants others to form a vaguely positive impression of her moral respectability. The goal is to receive a general form of admiration or respect for being "on the side of the angels." Other times, the grandstander wants something more specific. For example, she might want others to think she has morally respectable beliefs: her views about what counts as fairness or moral progress are truly something special. Or she might want others to be impressed by her sensitivity when it comes to moral issues: few others are as saddened by earthquakes or as outraged by minimum wage laws as she is. Or perhaps a grandstander wants others to think she has impeccable moral priorities: her Twitter followers might care mostly about lowering their tax burden, but she cares first and foremost about justice. Sometimes a grandstander might want to impress others with her moral insight about how to solve a problem: everyone needs to see that she knows exactly what causes extreme poverty and what must be done about it.

We can also think about what grandstanders want by framing their desires in terms of social status. Psychologists argue that there are two ways to attain social status: prestige and dominance.[6] Prestige refers to the status that comes from people thinking well of you for your knowledge, skills, or success. You have access to important resources that others don't, so they treat you with deference. In ancient times, this might mean knowing how to make a slingshot, or being a great hunter. In modern times, this might mean having expert knowledge of patent law, or being a world-class tennis player.

Dominance, on the other hand, refers to the status you get by instilling fear in others through intimidation, coercion, or even displays of brute force. The dominated treat you with deference because they fear being treated harshly. Our ancestors gained dominance by beating up or killing rival mating partners. In modern times, people still use physical violence, but we can also gain dominance by embarrassing others on social media, or lashing out at a colleague in a meeting.

This distinction between prestige and dominance can help us think about what motivates grandstanders. Grandstanders seek to elevate their social station, at least within some relevant social network. Often, they do this by seeking prestige for their moral qualities. They want the reputation for being inspiring moral exemplars, for example. They want this reputation, not necessarily for *doing* anything that is actually morally heroic, but for simply typing on their keyboard or uttering certain words. They think having this prestige will result in deference from others, at least when it comes to matters of morality.

But some grandstanders use moral talk for darker purposes. They grandstand to dominate others. They use moral talk to shame or silence others and create fear. They verbally threaten and seek to humiliate. They try to impress people by derogating their rivals, an all-too-common human impulse.[7] Instead of seeking status by trying to elevate their own prestige, they seek status by taking others down a notch. "Shut up and submit to my view of the world or I'll shame and embarrass you! I'm the morally good one here!" While grandstanders are usually after moral prestige, some are also out for domination.

The prestige/dominance aspects of grandstanding are supported by empirical work we have done on this topic.[8] In studies of college students and adults in the United States, moral grandstanding is consistently associated with one or both of the two functions. The prestige function is measured by how strongly people agree or disagree with statements like "My moral/political beliefs should be inspiring to others." The dominance function is measured by how strongly people agree or disagree with statements like "I share my moral/political beliefs to make people who disagree with me feel bad."

Who are grandstanders trying to impress? It depends. Sometimes, grandstanders hope to gain the esteem of like-minded peers. The people who roughly share your views about religion, politics, or economics are your "in-group." A grandstander might, for example, seek recognition from members of her in-group for being on the "right side" of some issue. In other cases, however, the grandstander will want members of an out-group to think of her as being eminently morally respectable. She might, for example, want people she disagrees with to recognize her superior moral judgment and defer to her in moral discourse as a result. Grandstanding aimed at an out-group is also more likely to be an attempt at domination. In our preliminary empirical work, we have found that the dominance form of grandstanding strongly tends to be out-group targeted.[9] In still other cases, a person might direct her grandstanding at a general audience, with no intention of discriminating among groups. She simply wants her audience to think favorably of her because of her moral qualities.

Let's now turn to the second part of our Basic Account: the Grandstanding Expression.

The Grandstanding Expression

When people grandstand, they do so by saying or writing something. A politician who wants voters to think that she cares more about the poor than her opponent does will say something during a stump speech on the campaign trail. A graduate student who wants her peers to think she was the most upset about the election results will write something on Facebook or Twitter. We can call the thing that the grandstander says or writes, the Grandstanding Expression. Grandstanders offer their Grandstanding Expression to get people to believe that they are morally special. To put it another way: grandstanders have a desire for recognition, and they say what they do to try to satisfy it. The politician and graduate student are attempting to get others to believe that they are morally respectable.

Human beings rarely act on the basis of a single motive. You might order edamame because you like the way it tastes *and* because you want to eat healthy food. Acts of grandstanding are no different. The grandstanding politician might want the electorate to think he cares deeply about the poor, but he might also want to rile up the crowd or embarrass his opponent. He might want others to be impressed with his unparalleled commitment to workers' rights *and* hope that, after hearing what he says, others will take action to support the labor movement.

So the Recognition Desire doesn't have to be the *only* thing motivating the Grandstanding Expression. We don't even think it must be the strongest motivation. But it does have to be strong. Just how strong? Strong enough that if the grandstander were to discover that her audience wasn't impressed with her moral qualities because of what she said, she would be disappointed. This doesn't mean that she actually has to find out whether people were impressed in order to engage in grandstanding. It's just a test of whether her desire is strong enough.

You might be thinking: but aren't we always disappointed when we don't get what we want? We don't think so. Sometimes we have relatively weak desires for things. And when we don't get them, we say, "Oh well," and move on. Brandon may want a baseball team from the National League to win the World Series next year, but he won't be *disappointed* if this doesn't happen. He's not sufficiently invested in it. It's simply a weak desire of his: he thinks, "It would be nice if it happened." The same could be true of wanting to impress others: failing to satisfy a very weak desire to impress others doesn't rise to the level of being disappointed were we to find out we didn't impress anyone. Grandstanders, on the other hand, would be disappointed if they found out they failed.

Why is disappointment a good test? The answer has to do with the way grandstanders are invested in impressing others. There's a sense in which we all want others to think highly of us. Typically, this desire is morally innocent and doesn't cause much damage because we are able to practice restraint and not act on it.[10] You might have a desire that guests at a dinner party know how much money you make. But you're probably able to control yourself and not blurt it out. It's when that desire is strong that it's harder to rein in. Grandstanders really want others to be impressed. That's why disappointment is a good test.

Grandstanders are in a tricky position. On the one hand, they cannot say just anything and expect people to come away thinking they are morally respectable. If you wanted someone to think you care deeply for the poor, it would make no sense to say something like:

"These pretzels are making me thirsty!"

On the other hand, rarely do grandstanders just come out and say something as direct as:

"I am the most morally sensitive person here, and I care more about the poor than the rest of you."

Instead, they will tend to say something more indirect:

"As someone who has long fought for the poor, I find all these proposals to eliminate rent control laws disgusting. If you think these are even worth listening to, you don't care about poverty in this country."

Although this piece of speech is much more vivid, the indirect approach doesn't explicitly say anything about how much the speaker cares about the poor. And yet the intended effect of a statement like that is to impress upon people this very fact. There is what the grandstander *says*. And there is what the grandstander tries to *imply*.[11] Typically, grandstanders try to imply something about themselves without just coming out and saying it. Indirect language like this is ubiquitous.[12] For example, when we make requests, we say things like: "If you could pass the salt, that'd be fantastic." And when we offer a bribe, we say: "Well officer, do you think there's any way to deal with this ticket right now?"

Some readers will be familiar with another form of indirect speech, humble-bragging: braggadocio wrapped in humble or complaining language. "Amazon won't let me order more than three copies of my book at a time. Is there some kind of limit on best-sellers? Annoying!"[13] "Why does my boss always assign me to the most important clients?" Humble-braggers are trying to show off. But they also try to cloak their true intentions in unassuming language. Grandstanders use indirect language for similar reasons.

But why do grandstanders use roundabout language that might fail to communicate the very thing they want others to believe? We don't know that there is a single explanation. Perhaps different contexts call for indirect speech for different reasons. Steven Pinker, Martin Nowak, and James Lee suggest several potential explanations for indirect speech that might account for why grandstanders are so drawn to it. We will discuss just one of them here.

One potential reason grandstanders use indirect language is that it gives them plausible deniability. There is a general social proscription against touting your alleged great qualities in public. Just as it would be gauche to announce that you have the best gustatory sensibilities or the most enlightened musical taste, it is socially unacceptable simply to state that you are morally impressive. But since this is exactly what grandstanders want to communicate, they need to exploit language to say it indirectly. By not coming out and directly announcing their moral greatness, they secure plausible deniability. You can even imagine someone being accused of grandstanding and replying: "Whoa, this is *not* about *me*. I'm sorry that I think repealing rent control laws really is *that* evil." Since there are social costs to obvious self-aggrandizement, grandstanders give themselves a way of denying what they are up to. Yet the fact that they use indirect language suggests that they often know what they are doing is gauche.

In context, though, it often seems obvious that someone is grandstanding even if she is using indirect speech. What is the point of using indirect speech, then? Notice that it's difficult to make up a sentence that is both an obvious case of grandstanding and also something that someone might actually say in ordinary conversation. This is because much of the evidence you use to conclude that someone is grandstanding involves context: the person's character and personality, his history of moral talk, the topic being discussed, his tone of voice, the contributions that others have made to the present discussion, and so on.[14] These clues are important because grandstanding involves the desire to impress others, and it's hard to know what is in someone else's head. All that contextual evidence, together with what the person says, can suggest they have the Recognition Desire.

So you might rightly conclude that someone is grandstanding because you have the help of contextual clues. But here's the key: usually, indirect speech that is taken out of context will not clearly indicate that a person is grandstanding. Yet direct speech would. Pulled from context, "I am the most morally sensitive person here . . . " is still damning. "As someone who has long fought for the poor . . ." outside of context is less so. Hence, there is an incentive to use indirect speech even when it doesn't provide cover in context. Of course, none of this means that grandstanders are always successful in pulling off the act of relative subtlety. The point is just that they have good reason to try.

DO GRANDSTANDERS THINK THEY ARE MORALLY RESPECTABLE?

Grandstanders try to get others to think of them as morally respectable. Sometimes they want to be thought of as one of the gang. Other times, they want to be thought of as morally exceptional. Either way, they usually want to be seen as morally better than others. But we have said nothing about whether grandstanders believe that they really are morally better than others. Must grandstanders think this?

In short, no. Imagine a politician who, in his speeches, feigns empathy for the plight of American factory workers because he wants voters to think that no one cares about them more than he does (and would be disappointed if they didn't come away thinking this). According to our account, this politician is grandstanding. Even though he doesn't really believe he's morally impressive, he wants others to think he is. However, we suspect that many grandstanders do think they are as morally great as they want you to believe. Understanding this can help us see why grandstanding is so common.

Chances are, you think you are better than most people at lots of things. Perhaps you think you are a better driver than most, or that you are more responsible, or a better parent. Chances are, you think that in many ways, you are better than the average person. Psychologists call the tendency to take such a flattering view of ourselves *self-enhancement*. Studies show, for example, that we tend to think we are more competent, more ambitious, more intelligent, and wiser than the average person.[15] We also think we work harder, are less prejudiced, are more upset by the events of 9/11, and care more about the environment than the average person.[16] In a particularly embarrassing finding for the authors and our colleagues, one study revealed that 90 percent of college professors say they are better than average teachers.[17] In general, we give ourselves pretty good grades.[18]

Interestingly, our self-enhancement is even stronger when it comes to morality. Studies show that we tend to rate our conduct as morally superior to the average person's.[19] We tend to think that we are more likely than others to do good, and less likely than others to do bad.[20] We also tend to think we are more likely to be honest and trustworthy.[21] Psychologists call this *moral self-enhancement*.[22] As psychologist David Dunning puts it, "people place themselves on moral pedestals that they deny their peers."[23] This tendency is not difficult to demonstrate empirically, either. According to psychologists Nadav Klein and Nicholas Epley, "Few biases in human judgment are easier to demonstrate than self-righteousness: the tendency to believe one is more moral than others."[24]

Let's consider just a few cases. In one study, 80 percent of participants said they would refuse to copy from a classmate's exam, but that only 55 percent of their peers would do so.[25] In another, 83 percent of participants said they would buy a flower to support a cancer research charity, but that only 56 percent of their peers would do so.[26] People tend to think they would feel worse than others after committing an unethical action, and they believe they are less capable of extreme unethical behavior than others are.[27] Even violent criminals think their behavior compares favorably to that of the rest of us. Prisoners rated themselves as above average for every pro-social trait except for law-abidingness, on which they modestly rated themselves as average.[28]

Furthermore, we rate ourselves as highly moral, not only relative to other people, but also in absolute terms.[29] Moral self-enhancement seems to be a universal human phenomenon, appearing in Eastern and Western cultures alike.[30] When it comes to morality, we tend to think of ourselves as pretty impressive specimens.

Psychologists call this flattering view of ourselves the *illusion of moral superiority*.[31] Why is it an illusion? For one, we can't *all* be better than average. But further, decades of research on moral character suggest that we aren't as virtuous as we think we are.[32] Our grandiose self-evaluations are likely mistaken. You are probably just morally average.[33] Remember how, in the study mentioned previously, 83 percent of students said they would buy a flower to support a cancer research charity, but only 56 percent of their peers would do so? After the charity drive, the students were surveyed: only 43 percent had bought a flower.[34]

Our moral self-conceptions are very important to us.[35] Much of our lives are spent attempting to control the impressions others form of us. These attempts are known in the psychological literature as "impression management."[36] If you think of yourself as a competent, hard-working employee, you will want others to think of you this way, too. So you try to cultivate that impression of yourself in your colleagues. You might always try to look busy, for example. In all kinds of ways, we try to project a positive image of ourselves. We make sure the barista at the coffee shop sees our tip. We display Auden and Dickens but hide our pulp romance novels. Shakespeare was right that we treat the world as a stage.

It is no surprise, then, that we care deeply about our moral reputations and go to great lengths to curate and protect them.[37] Andrew Vonasch and colleagues performed a study that revealed just how much we care what others think of our moral qualities.[38] They found that many people would prefer to spend a year in jail, lose a hand, or even die before being known as a criminal in their community, being assumed to be a Neo-Nazi, or falsely thought to be a pedophile. Many subjects chose to stick a hand into a bowl of writhing, wriggling, beetle larvae to prevent the larger university community from learning that they had received a (doctored) high "racism" score on an implicit association test (IAT).

If it is important to your self-conception that you are morally great, you'll want others to know this, too. No wonder so many people go out of their way in public discourse to get others to believe what they already believe about themselves: that they are morally exceptional. In other words, it should be no surprise that people are motivated to grandstand.

WITTING AND UNWITTING GRANDSTANDING

According to the Basic Account, grandstanders are trying to satisfy the Recognition Desire. In many cases, a grandstander will *consciously* attempt to satisfy that desire. Psychologists tell us that some of our impression management is indeed conscious.[39] Someone might think to herself: "I'd like these people to be impressed by my commitment to justice, so I'll say something like this . . ." We can call this *witting grandstanding:* the grandstander knows that she's trying to call attention to her moral qualities (even if she wouldn't describe what she's doing as "grandstanding").

Grandstanding doesn't have to be witting, though. Sometimes we do things to satisfy desires even though we aren't thinking, "I should do something to satisfy this desire of mine." For example, you probably want healthy teeth. Because you want this, you brush your teeth. But you rarely think to yourself, "I want healthy teeth, so I'll brush them." Of course, you are still brushing to satisfy a desire for healthy teeth. You just aren't thinking of that desire. Something similar can happen with grandstanding. You might have the Recognition Desire, try to satisfy it with a Grandstanding Expression, but not consciously think: "I will say this because I want people to be impressed by my moral excellence."[40]

A critic might object: "If someone is not *consciously* trying to impress others with her moral talk, then she cannot be grandstanding. If you asked her why she made her high-minded moral pronouncement, her explanation would be simply that she cares for the poor, or the downtrodden American factory worker. But that is not grandstanding!"

This response assumes a naïve view about how well we know our own minds. In a famous experiment, psychologists Richard Nisbett and Timothy Wilson had subjects select from a range of stockings. Interestingly, subjects consistently chose the stockings on the far-right side. When they were asked why they picked those particular stockings, they didn't say that they picked them because of their position. They said they chose them based on their felt quality or their color, even when the stockings were identical. They simply looked for—or invented—reasons to rationalize their choice.[41] Psychologists call this confabulation.[42] Because our true motivations are often not transparent—even to ourselves—we confabulate explanations for our behavior. When we confabulate, we tell stories that cohere with our overall self-conception. For instance, we might tell ourselves that we chose the stockings because we recognize the finer things in life, and those stockings were simply finer. Since we give ourselves high moral grades, it is not surprising that we cast our reasons for engaging in moral talk in a flattering light. It makes us feel good and important. Although we tell ourselves we are using moral talk for admirable purposes, there may still be more suspect motives lurking underneath.

Everyday life is full of examples of confabulation. In their book, *The Elephant in the Brain*, Kevin Simler and Robin Hanson suggest the following cases:

> Parents will often enforce kids' bedtimes "for their own good," when a self-serving motive seems just as likely—that parents simply want an hour or two of peace and quiet without the kids. Of course, many parents genuinely believe that bedtimes are good for their children, but that belief is self-serving enough that we should be skeptical that it's the full story.

> People who download copyrighted material—songs, books, movies—often rationalize their actions by saying, "Faceless corporations take most of the profits from artists anyway." The fact that most of these people wouldn't dream of stealing CDs or DVDs from Best Buy (an equally faceless corporate entity) attests to a different explanation for their behavior, which is that online, they feel anonymous and are less afraid of getting caught.[43]

We suggest another:

> People who make high-minded moral pronouncements on social media and use moral talk to shame and silence people often explain their behavior by saying they are standing up for the oppressed or defending what is right. But these same people probably wouldn't speak this way in a private face-to-face conversation. This suggests that what these people really want is to use their public platform to garner moral prestige, or worse, to dominate others for social benefits.

Put simply, we may often be self-deceived about our true motives for contributing to public discourse. We sometimes grandstand without knowing it. Why does this happen? Psychologist William von Hippel and evolutionary biologist Robert Trivers argue that humans evolved to deceive themselves about their own motives in situations where consciously acting on those motives could reveal what they are up to, thereby undermining their goals.[44] One reason we are often unaware of our own self-enhancement motives is that we evolved to suppress them. It makes sense. Knowingly trying to impress others can lead you to engage in clumsy behavior that is transparently self-serving and thus ineffective. If you've observed first dates at coffee shops, you've probably overheard this kind of self-enhancement. It tends to backfire. But if our self-enhancing motives are hidden from conscious view, we can be more cunning in how we go about impressing others. This self-deception has an added bonus: when we are called out for grandstanding, we can deny it with a clear conscience. After all, you didn't *think* you were trying to impress others.

Some grandstanding is certainly witting. We knowingly try to puff ourselves up with public pronouncements aimed at displaying our moral righteousness. But, depressing as it might be, unwitting grandstanding is probably more common than many people suppose.

We said at the beginning of the book that you may have questions and doubts along the way, and we may have hit such a point already, having laid out our Basic Account. So let's explore some possible questions and objections before we go further.

GRANDSTANDING AND FALSEHOOD

Accusations of grandstanding usually come from ideological opponents, who presumably also think what the supposed grandstander is saying is false. Perhaps as a result, some people think that if someone is grandstanding, what she is saying must be false. But that is a mistake.

Nothing about grandstanding requires that grandstanders say false things. Of course, grandstanders may want you to believe that they are morally enlightened, and *that* may be false. But what they actually *say* may be true. You can imagine a grandstander posting something like this on Facebook, as one of the authors once did:

> No one should die because they cannot afford health care, and no one should go broke because they get sick. We are only as strong as the weakest among us. If you agree, please post this as your Facebook or Myspace status for the rest of the day.

Although this is a strange artifact from simpler times on the internet, there is nothing obviously mistaken in this statement. Every moral claim in it could very well be true. Yet that does not exempt it from serving as a Grandstanding Expression—which it was. (We should know.)

If you are still skeptical, look back at Harvey Weinstein's statement in chapter 1. As far as we know everything he said is true, and yet this should make no difference to your assessment that he did some Grade-A grandstanding. The point is simple, but important: it is not a defense against the charge of grandstanding to point out that what you say is true. You can speak the truth *and* grandstand.

Of course, grandstanders often do say false things. In fact, as we will show in the next chapter, some of the social dynamics of status seeking in public discourse encourage grandstanders to do precisely that.

DOES GRANDSTANDING WORK?

Grandstanders use moral talk to look good. They want you to think they are morally respectable. But are people taken in by the act? Is grandstanding an effective way of shaping your reputation? We in the audience know that moral talk can be exploited for personal gain, and we recognize many instances of grandstanding, if not all of them. Many of us roll our eyes at grandstanders, or text our coauthors to say, "He's at it again." But often grandstanding does work, which helps explain why so many people do it. Especially skilled grandstanders can convince lots of people that they are moral exemplars. Why does grandstanding work? And why does it sometimes fail? These questions need to be studied empirically, but we can say a few things here.

Let's start with why grandstanding might work. We typically assume that others are not deceiving us.[45] Social life would be very difficult if you couldn't rely on others to be truthful. According to sociologist Erving Goffman, we generally expect that "an individual who implicitly or explicitly signifies that he has certain social characteristics ought in fact to be what he claims he is."[46] When people use moral language to signify they are morally special, they do so against the background presumption that people generally present themselves accurately. Grandstanding may be successful simply because we tend to take people at their word.

But grandstanders often fail to convince others of their moral goodness. For example, we doubt that the Harvey Weinstein statement we discussed in chapter 1 convinced anyone that he is a good person (or perhaps even a decent person). So what explains whether grandstanding succeeds or fails? There are lots of potential explanations. We will suggest two.

First, your grandstanding will be less successful if the image you are trying to project is inconsistent with what your audience already believes about you. People won't be impressed by someone's grandstanding if they already think she's a bad person. In other words, an audience is less likely to buy a speaker's grandstanding when they suspect her of hypocrisy. This is one reason why Weinstein's grandstanding was such an abject failure. His widely reported bad behavior was too incongruous with his protestation that he is one of the good guys. Once the audience sees discrepancies between the moral image a grandstander wants to project and her actual moral qualities, they will actually think less of her.[47] People have a low tolerance for hypocrisy.[48]

Second, grandstanding is successful to the extent your audience already shares your moral beliefs and values. The more different they are from you, the less likely it is that you will impress them. At the 2017 Golden Globe Awards, actress Meryl Streep gave a widely discussed speech criticizing President-elect Trump. She began:

> Please sit down. Thank you. I love you all. You'll have to forgive me. I lost my voice in screaming and lamentation this week.[49]

In the speech that followed, she cast the recent election result as a hateful attack on Hollywood's progressive values, "foreigners," and the press. We can't be certain that Streep was grandstanding, but for the sake of illustration, let's assume she was. Reactions to her speech were polarized. If you already agreed with Streep's generally progressive values and her beliefs about Trump's election—like virtually everyone in the room with her—then you probably thought she was taking a bold and courageous stand for justice. Actress Laverne Cox tweeted: "Everything she said. Thank you #MerylStreep for [your] work and everything you said tonight. #empathy #GoldenGlobes."[50] Comedian Retta tweeted "A broad to be emulated. #MerylStreep."[51] Musician Mark Ronson: "I repeat, Meryl Streep is the greatest."[52]

On the other hand, if you strongly disagree with Streep's values and beliefs, you were likely unimpressed. You might agree with one critic that Streep's "moralizing hypocrisy" is "typical of self-congratulatory Hollywood."[53] These widely divergent reactions to the same speech suggest that the more your audience agrees with you, the more likely they are to be impressed by your grandstanding.

Now that we know some of the factors that influence whether grandstanding works, let's turn our attention to the important question of who grandstands. Is it more common in some groups than others?

IS GRANDSTANDING JUST A "LEFT-WING PROBLEM"?

At least in the United States and United Kingdom, public accusations of grandstanding have disproportionately been leveled by the political right against the left, and particularly against the progressive left. However, some circles of progressives are also concerned about the grandstanders in their midst. As Jane Coaston writes in *The New York Times Magazine*,

> It's not difficult to find, in conversations among progressives, widespread eye-rolling over a certain type of person: the one who will take a heroic stance on almost any issue—furious indignation over the casting of a live-action "Aladdin" film, vehement defense of Hillary Clinton's fashion choices, extravagant emotional investment in the plight of a group to which the

speaker does not belong—in what feels like a transparent bid for
the praise, likes and aura of righteousness that follows.[54]

Due to popular beliefs about who is most guilty of grandstanding,
you might have picked up this book anticipating a jeremiad about
the woeful state of politics on the left. If that describes your expectations, you may have noticed that our Basic Account is, in an important sense, perfectly general. It makes no reference to the political
content of a grandstander's beliefs, because there could be—and
have been—grandstanders of all political persuasions. Our psychological profile of grandstanders is general in the same way. The
psychological mechanisms that contribute to grandstanding behavior are general human traits, not limited to the members of any
one group.

A brief tour of political history confirms that grandstanding is not
limited to the contemporary left. Thinking just of the United States,
before this apparent awakening of grandstanding on the left, there
was grandstanding about national security after the 9/11 attacks
and during the Iraq War, as American politicians took every opportunity to show that they were not "soft on terror." The low point for
ridiculous grandstanding in this phase came when Republican con-
gressperson Bob Ney had congressional cafeterias change the name
of French fries to "freedom fries" in response to France's opposition
to the invasion of Iraq. Before this came the Clinton sex scandal,
which prompted endless grandstanding and moralizing from the
right about sexual morality and fitness to lead. Earlier in that decade
the left renewed its interest in political correctness, a movement that
began under that name in America in the 1970s. Perhaps the high-
watermark for grandstanding from the right in our lifetimes came
during the reign of the Moral Majority, the major figures of which
built national reputations for their public displays of moral piety.

And of course, before all of this came the Red Scare, during which those in the public eye competed for the title of most fervid anti-Communist, and bullied others into playing along.

It is interesting to speculate about why the reputation for being the worst grandstanders bounces around between groups and political affiliations. It does not seem to track being in political power, and it is clearly not confined to any ideology or party affiliation. Furthermore, honest people can recognize that their own side does it.

These remarks about the distribution of grandstanding are supported by preliminary social scientific work we have undertaken.[55] We mentioned earlier that our studies suggest people grandstand to seek prestige status and dominance status. These same studies suggest that grandstanding—particularly when aimed at acquiring prestige—is relatively common and widespread. Furthermore, we found that particular political affiliations are not associated with either prestige grandstanding or dominance grandstanding. In other words, grandstanding does not seem to be more associated with either left-leaning or right-leaning beliefs. Democrats and Republicans are equally likely to grandstand, as are liberals and conservatives. Interestingly, however, we found that people who hold more extreme political views (whether right or left) are more likely to grandstand for prestige than centrists. But this is not so for dominance grandstanding. In other words, whereas those on the extreme sides of the political spectrum are more likely to grandstand for prestige, there is roughly the same amount of dominance grandstanding across the political spectrum.

So, in sum, and despite currently popular perceptions of the matter, grandstanding is not just a left-wing problem. Rather, it is fairly common behavior. But people who hold extreme political views are more likely to grandstand to raise their prestige status than are those with more moderate views.

ARE WE GRANDSTANDING?

From the moment many saw the title of this book, they turned their attention to us, the authors, and worried that *we* might be guilty of grandstanding. The thought goes something like this: if we're writing a whole book filled with moral talk, telling people how badly they behave in public discourse and claiming that we know a better way, aren't we trying to make ourselves look good? Aren't we just grandstanding?

If this is your reaction, we have to admit, we're flattered by the attention. Even so, if someone took this to be a tough objection to the book even after thinking it through, it would be a little disappointing. Because even if we are horrible grandstanders, our arguments might still be good ones. Whether we're also good people just isn't relevant to whether we're right about grandstanding. Think of it this way: pretend that this book was written by an unbelievably clever robot who has been observing social media. You could evaluate the robot's arguments without worrying about any further facts about it. You can, and should, do the same for us. Still, we get it. It might be important to you for some reason to believe that this book is an act of grandstanding. We could resist the charge. Of course, our denial would have little evidential value for someone who already doubts our motives. You would thus simply respond that you don't believe our reports about whether we are moved by the Recognition Desire. But now we are locked in an endless struggle of accusations and denials with no end in sight. This useless back and forth is good evidence for a general suggestion we will argue for later: we shouldn't go around accusing people of grandstanding.

At any rate, we think the truth or falsity of our theory of grandstanding is much more interesting than whether we ourselves are grandstanders. Which, of course, is just what a couple of grandstanders *would* say.

WHAT ABOUT "VIRTUE SIGNALING"?

A few years after we started writing about grandstanding, we noticed people using the term "virtue signaling." The two ideas are clearly related, and we suspect that people use the phrases interchangeably. Labels generally don't matter that much. What we are interested in, after all, is the idea to which a label refers. But sometimes one label does a better job of promoting understanding and limiting confusion than does an alternative label. We think this is one such case, so let us say a few words about why grandstanding is a better term for the phenomenon in which we are interested.

As far as we can tell, the term "virtue signaling" entered popular vernacular in 2015.[56] Much of its current usage involves complaints from the political right about the behavior of the political left (and criticisms of the right from the left for criticizing them in this way). The term has no doubt become politically charged. We think it is best not to use it, not only for this reason, but also because the term can be misleading.

"Signaling," as a concept used in biology and psychology, does not necessarily involve *attempts* or *desires* to communicate. Signals are behaviors or features of an organism that either intentionally communicate information, or were selected for through evolution because they communicate information that makes the organism more fit. Peacocks have long trains of feathers that signal fitness to females: the bigger the train, the more fit for survival (you have to be healthy and strong to lug that thing around), and therefore the better the mate.[57] But the peacock has not *attempted to* grow these feathers for this purpose. Many toxic insects are brightly colored. This tells prey to avoid them. Their coloration is a signal, but again, not one they are trying to send.[58]

Human beings send some signals intentionally. For instance, some people drive expensive cars because they want others to think they are wealthy. But many human behaviors send signals whether we mean to do so or not. Shopping at Whole Foods, driving a Prius, and listening to NPR can signal things about you, even if you aren't aware of it. We can also be mistaken about whether we are signaling. Economist Bryan Caplan argues that while most people think that our education system serves primarily to create knowledgeable, skilled, and well-rounded adults, this is not so.[59] According to Caplan, the primary function of the education system—and especially colleges and universities—is to signal to potential employers how intelligent and conscientious you are, as well as how good you are at conforming to the expectations of others. This is exactly what modern employers look for: competent, hard-working team players. Yet who goes to college knowing that having a degree shows employers you're a competent, hard-working team player? We didn't.

So whereas much signaling is unintentional, the phenomenon we refer to as grandstanding involves wanting or attempting to get others to think something about you. Yet since so much signaling happens without wanting or attempting to send a signal, we think the term "virtue signaling" can be misleading. So we opt against using it.

"Virtue signaling" is misleading for another reason. Notice that when we say "X signals Y" we often mean that X actually has Y. For example, suppose we said, "Having a graduate degree signals literacy and the economic freedom to devote six years of your life to study." Under normal circumstances, we would say this because we want to communicate that those things are true of people with graduate degrees. So to say that someone is virtue signaling can mistakenly imply that the person actually *is* virtuous. But, of course, most accusations of virtue signaling are not meant to suggest that the person actually has virtue.

Here's another potential source of confusion. The term "virtue signaling" implies that one is signaling (or trying to signal) one's *virtue*. Virtue is normally thought of as excellence of character. But as we explained earlier in the chapter, one can grandstand without trying to get others to think that one has excellent character. One might simply want others to think that one is minimally morally decent (where most others fall well below even that standard). "Grandstanding" carries no implication that one is trying to get others to recognize specifically one's virtue.

Relatedly, the term "virtue signaling" inspires some to talk of "vice signaling." "Vice signaling" supposedly involves boasting about what a bad person you are. Hardcore libertarians, for example, might "vice signal" about how little they care about the plight of the poor. It seems to us, however, that "vice signaling" is better understood as just another way of grandstanding with an eye to impressing your in-group with the "correct" moral values (Ayn Rand fans would cheer you on) or denigrating your out-group, who have the "incorrect" moral values (those who fecklessly defend the weak and lazy). Moreover, if discussion of "vice signaling" continues to catch on, we can look forward to lots of pointless arguments about whether someone is "virtue signaling" or "vice signaling," depending on whether they are expressing good or bad values. We think the term should be avoided entirely.

Finally, people often accuse others of virtue signaling because they suspect the putative signaler does not actually believe the moral claim she is making. In other words, the charge is that the accused is engaging in insincere cheap talk. They are merely signaling, at no cost to themselves, that other people should be subjected to some moral demand that they don't even believe in. This fixation on insincerity is myopic, and it causes people to overlook other problems that arise from using moral talk for self-promotion. As we will see, some of the most serious problems with moral grandstanding occur because grandstanders *are* so often sincere. Of course, grandstanders are sometimes insincere, too. You can grandstand whether you actually believe what you say or not.

Perhaps none of these concerns individually is sufficient reason to reject the term "virtue signaling." But together, they show that the term can be highly misleading. Why not simply avoid it?

We should admit, though, that there is one arena of moral self-promotion where "virtue signaling" appears to be the better term: non-linguistic behaviors. Suppose, for, example, that Tosi wants people to think that he cares deeply about the environment. He might buy and drive a Prius. It sounds awkward to call this grandstanding. "Virtue signaling" seems to be the better term here, though it will still be potentially misleading in some of the ways we noted. But because this book is about the use and abuse of moral *talk*, we won't worry much about non-linguistic forms of moral preening.

CONCLUSION

Grandstanding is the use of moral talk for self-promotion. According to our Basic Account of the phenomenon, it involves a desire (of a certain strength) that others think well of you for your moral qualities, and a contribution to public discourse designed to satisfy that desire. You don't have to know you're grandstanding in order to grandstand, nor do you have to say anything false. We've said a lot in this chapter about the general features of grandstanding.

But our discussion so far has been a bit abstract. It would also be helpful to know what grandstanding usually looks like in the wild. In the next chapter, we offer help with exactly that: a field guide to grandstanding.

Chapter 3

Grandstanding: A Field Guide

Attempts to impress others are common in social life. Often, this has nothing to do with morality. Some people, for example, try to impress others with their intelligence. One way of doing this is to correct other people's statements. Your friend remarks that K2 is the second-tallest mountain on earth. You interject: "Yes, but only by elevation. By prominence, it isn't even in the top 20." Some sprinkle unnecessary details in their stories to hint at their intelligence. In the midst of a story about her wisdom teeth extraction, a colleague nonchalantly mentions that her surgery happened the same week she netted a perfect LSAT score. Some leave a paper trail, by collecting advanced degrees. Others burst into a dissertation defense exclaiming, "I'm sorry I'm late, but Stravinsky was playing on NPR and I simply had to finish listening!" One teenager who grew up to be a philosophy professor at Harvard used to carry a copy of Plato's *Republic* around Brooklyn with the cover facing out.[1] A moderately clever person could spend a lifetime devising ways to make sure others get the right idea about how smart he is.

The same is true of grandstanding. People use moral talk in creative ways to get others to think they are morally impressive. In the last chapter, we gave a general psychological explanation of *why* people grandstand. In this chapter, we will discuss *how* people grandstand.

We identify five common ways people grandstand: piling on, ramping up, trumping up,[2] displays of strong emotions, and dismissiveness. Along the way, we use research in psychology to explain why grandstanding takes these forms.

But first, we want to preempt a natural misunderstanding. This chapter contains a field guide to grandstanding. We will show you why grandstanding often takes the form of, for example, excessive moral outrage. But we do not claim that every time someone displays excessive outrage, she is therefore grandstanding. We are not offering a *test* for determining whether someone is grandstanding. Think again of the person who collects advanced degrees to impress people with her intelligence. For some people, that really is the primary reason to collect degrees. But it would obviously be a mistake to conclude that *everyone* who collects advanced degrees is just trying to show off how smart they are. Some people might just enjoy being in school, for instance.

Our goal, then, is to show you what grandstanding often looks like. It is not to give you a foolproof method for positively identifying instances of grandstanding.

PILING ON

Many of us have found ourselves trapped in meetings that seem to go on forever. A common reason for interminable meetings is the repetition of what has already been said. Why do people speak up just to say something that has been ably expressed already, maybe even several times? Perhaps they haven't been paying close attention. Or they instead just want to be seen as having made an important contribution in some way, even if it is only to promote someone else's idea. They might just want to be seen as a team player, an agreeable co-worker, or as someone whose thinking is in line with the organization's values. Whatever their reasons, we are stuck there, distracted from our actual work until they get it out of their systems.

Sometimes moral talk seems to follow the model of the long meeting. People chime in on discussions of moral issues effectively to say nothing more than "yeah!" We call this phenomenon "piling on." As the name suggests, it occurs when someone contributes to public moral discourse to do nothing more than proclaim her agreement with something that has already been said. When people grandstand by piling on, they are just trying to get in on the action or register their inclusion on the right side. They can do this in any number of ways. Someone might pile on by rehashing someone else's earlier remark, by repeating it word for word, or simply by noting that she agrees with what everyone else has been saying.

Piling on is perhaps most easily observed in internet discussions. For example, suppose that numerous posters in a discussion thread have already argued passionately that a petition should be started to protest some injustice. The intentions of the group are already abundantly clear, and the matter is no longer up for debate. Yet someone adds the following:

> I want to echo what others have said. This petition is vital to the cause of justice and I happily and wholeheartedly support it. We need to show that we are on the right side of history. I cannot wait to sign!

Piling on also sometimes involves much darker behavior, as when people on social media momentarily focus their bile on a single violator of some putative norm and everyone publicly blames and shames her. Naturally, this continues until the pilers-on succeed in extracting some statement of remorse from their target, at which point the statement is inevitably deemed "too little, too late" and picked apart for new infractions, about which more piling on occurs.

For a real-world example of piling on, consider the case of Keziah Daum, a white teenager who shared pictures on social media of herself in a traditional tight-fitting Chinese dress that she wore to prom. One user commented on her photos, "my culture is NOT your goddamn prom dress," a war-cry to pile onto Daum for cultural appropriation. That comment was subsequently retweeted more than forty thousand times.[3]

It makes perfect sense that grandstanding takes the form of piling on. If you want others to think of you as sharing the values of your preferred group, an obvious strategy for satisfying this desire is to register your view publicly, even if doing so contributes nothing to the discussion. Adding your own condemnation to a shaming pile-on is a simple, low-cost way of broadcasting your moral beliefs.

Grandstanders who pile on in such cases are trying to make clear that they are on the Correct Side. In many cases, the grandstander genuinely believes that the target is guilty, and deserves to be shamed. It just so happens that what morality requires of her also coincides with a chance to prove her moral credentials.

But there is good reason to think that some grandstanders who pile on are uncertain, or even downright skeptical, that the target *du jour* deserves to be pilloried. Yet they contribute to the pile-on anyway to appear morally respectable to their peers.

Social psychologists have long known that people frequently express agreement with the public pronouncements of their group even when they privately disagree. Pioneering social psychologist Solomon Asch showed precisely this in his famous work on conformity.[4] In his most well-known experiment, a lone participant was placed in a group with several actors who behaved according to a script set by the experimenter. (Psychologists call these actors "confederates.") The confederates gave intentionally (and clearly) inaccurate answers about the relative length of lines displayed to the group. Participants often expressed agreement with the inaccurate claims (about 36 percent of the time), even when they later admitted that they did not agree.[5]

Even in a highly contrived low-stakes environment, on a mundane question, people were loath to "make waves," as one participant put it, by disagreeing with the group. Other versions of the experiment involved planting one dissenting confederate along with the inaccurate majority, with the result that participants were more likely to express their actual beliefs.[6] Importantly, participants in that version of the experiment generally claimed that the presence of another dissenter did not make their own expression of dissent any easier. Yet dissent from the majority was more common with a fellow dissenter than without one. So we are not necessarily aware of how strongly we are affected by the pressure to conform.

Just as we want others to think we are competent judges of the length of lines, we also want our peers to think we are morally respectable. And so people who have private reservations about the justification for piling on will grandstand to get in on the action anyway.

Asch's conformity studies suggest that many grandstanders will go along with pile-ons even if they harbor private reservations. But lots of piling on involves nasty public shaming. Will people really go that far to prove they are on the Correct Side, even if they are unsure of whether the object of their bilious tirade has done anything wrong?[7]

In recent studies, sociologist Robb Willer and colleagues extended Asch's findings to show that people will indeed go further.[8] In one study, subjects rated one wine as much better than another (identical) wine due to social pressure, even though they privately judged the wines similarly. Many of these same subjects would then go on to publicly sanction a deviant member of the group who rated the wines equally. In other words, people punish others who deviate from what is thought to be a popular view, even though the punishers themselves don't actually agree with that view.[9] Willer and his colleagues call this the "false enforcement of norms." On its face, this is odd behavior. Why would people sanction others for holding a belief they themselves hold?

Willer and colleagues argue that when people tailor their public views to fit in and avoid criticism, they worry they will look insincere and opportunistic. But how do you convince others you are sincere even though you are just going along with the crowd? One way of seeming more serious about what you say is to put it into action—to walk the walk in addition to talking the talk. So private doubters have a natural solution: punish deviants.

If you go out of your way to sanction people who have the "wrong view," you make a more convincing case that you are a true believer. The result is a "self-reinforcing dynamic": people defend views to avoid criticism and then criticize others to avoid suspicion of insincerity. Others then see you punishing people for their "wrong views" and conclude they should go along, too, and in turn punish others. In some cases, large segments of apparently "true believers" might end up not only publicly endorsing a view they don't hold, but also punishing others for not holding it!

This account of norm enforcement can help explain some of the pile-ons you see on social media. How much moral talk is driven by people wanting to fit in? How many people were privately skeptical that wearing a traditional Chinese dress to prom qualified as harmful cultural appropriation, but went along with the pile-on because this is what they believe their group demands of them? It's hard to say.[10]

The pressure for a person to conform to the behavior of a group is even stronger when membership in that group is an important part of her social identity. This is true especially of new members of groups. In fraternities and sororities, for example, pledges judge themselves as fitting the stereotypes of their groups more closely early in the process than they do later on.[11] They conform, in other words, to feel like they match their self-conceptions as group members. It is easy to imagine people adopting and expressing moral beliefs that are viewed favorably within the group for similar reasons.

People who fail to conform adequately risk falling victim to what psychologists call the Black Sheep Effect.[12] Unsurprisingly, people judge the highest status members of their group more favorably than they do high status members of other groups. But people also judge low status or deviant members of their *own group* more negatively than they do similar members of other groups. This makes sense, if you think about it. You can admire diehard members of the opposing political party in at least one sense: even if they're wrong, they're principled. And even moderate members of the opposing party can be useful—they're actually pretty reasonable when they cross over to support policies you like. But "deviant" members of your own party need to get their act together. Don't they know what side they're on? Think, for instance, of how some staunch Republicans spoke about Senator John McCain when he criticized President Trump, or how the progressive wing of the Democratic Party talks about President Clinton and the center-left agenda his administration pursued in the 1990s. In both cases, you can see the Black Sheep Effect at work.

In other words, all else being equal, the worst thing you can be according to members of your group is the black sheep. Being the black sheep is even worse than never having belonged to the group in the first place. When people from your in-group are discussing a moral issue, the stakes are high. Even minor missteps can be a big deal and can throw your status in the group into question. Thus, it is often worthwhile to chime in and remind everyone that you are with them, even if you have reservations about what the group is doing.

Someone might object that we seem to be claiming that all statements of solidarity are cases of grandstanding. After all, when you show solidarity with a cause or a group of people, you make a moral claim—often one that adds nothing to what others have already said—simply to make your moral views known. The whole point of showing solidarity is to identify yourself publicly as a supporter of some disadvantaged person or group, for instance, so that people recognize that you hold that position. But surely there is nothing wrong with showing one's solidarity with a worthy cause. So if our account condemns such statements as typical manifestations of grandstanding, that is a problem.

We agree that many statements of solidarity are laudable, and that it would be incorrect to describe them as grandstanding. The type of solidarity statements we have in mind are those motivated primarily by a desire to help those with whom the speaker is in solidarity. In such cases, it is a misleading and incomplete description of the speaker's motivation to say simply that she is hoping to be recognized as having a certain moral view. Crucially, she is hoping to attain that recognition *in order to help others*. Such a person would presumably feel disappointed—and maybe even a little guilty—if she were the only person to benefit from what she said. A grandstander, on the other hand, would not be so chagrinned. Indeed, a grandstander would be pleased to have gotten the recognition she was after, and disappointed if her attempt failed.[13]

RAMPING UP

In the latter half of the twentieth century, the Soviets and Americans were locked in a nuclear arms race. By the early 1980s, each side had stockpiled tens of thousands of warheads.[14] What drove the arms race? A desire to avoid being outpaced by the other side.[15] After producing each new bomb, the Soviets did not say to themselves, "Yes, this is the correct number of bombs to have, we can stop now." Instead, they kept building bombs to keep up with and amass more warheads than the Americans. It was a competition. Each side was trying to outdo the other.

Moral talk often devolves into a moral arms race, where people make increasingly strong claims about the matter under discussion. Call this *ramping up*. When people ramp up, they are not trying to arrive at the correct moral claim any more than the Soviets and Americans were trying to produce the correct number of bombs. Instead, they are trying to outdo one another. What drives them is the desire to be the most morally impressive. So they use increasingly strong moral claims to signal that they are more attuned to matters of justice, and that others simply do not understand or appreciate the nuance or gravity of the situation.

Grandstanding often takes the form of ramping up. Consider the following sort of exchange:

ANN: We can all agree that the Senator's behavior was wrong and that she should be publicly censured.

BEN: Oh please—if we really cared about justice we should seek her removal from office. We simply cannot tolerate that sort of behavior and I will not stand for it.

CHIP: As someone who has long fought for social justice, I'm sympathetic to these suggestions, but does anyone know the criminal law on this issue? I want to suggest that we should pursue criminal charges. We would all do well to remember that the world is watching.

Why does grandstanding follow this pattern? People often imagine themselves as occupying a certain position in comparison to others. Psychologists call this "social comparison."[16] For example, we rate our attractiveness or sense of humor by reference to how attractive or funny other people are. As we saw in chapter 2, most of us think we are pretty morally impressive.

We often make these judgments about our relative moral purity before hearing what others believe. Once we hear what others' views are (or at least what they say they are), we have two options. We can either accept that we are morally ordinary and keep our views as they are, or we can ever so slightly shift our views (or at least our presentation of them) to retain our status as the moral exemplar within the group. For many, the latter option is preferable. And so what once seemed like a reasonable view must now be exchanged for something a bit more morally exacting.

Look back at the earlier conversation to see how this might play out. Before this discussion started, Ann, Ben, and Chip might have each considered themselves to be morally respectable about matters of justice. But then Ann spoke her piece. Once Ann offers her moral diagnosis, Ben and Chip now must make a move to retain their perceived position within the group. They must up the ante, or else look like they were bested by someone with superior moral credentials. Ben and Chip's grandstanding will tend to push the group's views toward one extreme. And were Ann herself to chime in again, she may end up shifting her own view to maintain the image she wishes to project. She was in favor of pursuing criminal charges all along, you see. It just seemed so obvious that she didn't think to mention it.

Although our example of ramping up utilizes increasingly strong critical reactions, ramping up may also result in increasingly strong positive claims. One person may describe someone's behavior as "brave and worthy of our admiration," whereas another may claim that "this act was not only brave, but the most courageous and self-less act I have ever witnessed." Here, too, ramping up can be used to communicate that one is morally respectable—that one can iden-tify unjustly overlooked moral saints.

In a discussion between lots of people who are motivated by the Recognition Desire, we can even *expect* a moral arms race. Ramping up explains why so many conversations about morality and politics get out of hand so quickly. What begins as a disagreement about tariffs ends with someone calling a person with whom they agree about most moral questions a Nazi.

Do people really shift their public moral judgments to appear a certain way? It seems so. Psychologists Sarah Rom and Paul Conway showed that people will change their public (but not private) moral judgments depending on whether they think others are expecting them to display warmth, or instead competence.[17] We should not as-sume that every moral pronouncement people make on Facebook is their deeply held and carefully considered view. Many moral claims are made strategically, by people hoping to induce you to think of them a certain way.

Of course, not every "ramped-up" discussion is driven by grandstanding. Sometimes, people make stronger claims simply because they disagree with others and are trying to get closer to the truth of the matter. If you see someone give a lukewarm con-demnation of slavery, it would be fitting to interject with a stronger one. It can be difficult to tell whether you're observing people make stronger claims in good faith or instead watching a grandstanding-fueled moral arms race. But just because it's hard to tell the difference, that doesn't mean there isn't one.

TRUMPING UP

In the Hans Christian Andersen fairy tale, "The Princess and the Pea," a prince searches for a true princess to be his wife. Despite his best efforts, he repeatedly fails to find a suitable match. Then one night a young woman shows up at the town gate seeking shelter from a storm, claiming to be a real princess. After she is invited to stay, the queen tests the young woman's claim to royalty by placing a single pea under the pile of twenty mattresses and twenty feather beds on which the young woman is to sleep. In the morning, they ask how she slept. "Oh terribly badly!" she says. "I have hardly closed my eyes the whole night. Heaven knows what was in the bed. I seemed to be lying upon some hard thing, and my whole body is black and blue this morning. It's horrible!" The royal family realizes that they had found their princess, for "nobody but a real princess could have such . . . delicate skin."[18]

What makes this story amusing is that *of course* no one could be that sensitive. Andersen pokes fun at such a ridiculous test of sensitivity to establish royal credentials. Yet some people attempt to establish their *moral* credentials by displaying a similar degree of sensitivity to moral problems. Often this results in spurious claims about the presence of a moral problem where in fact there is none. We call this errant use of moral claims *trumping up*. Just as a prosecutor might trump up false charges against a suspect, participants in moral discourse sometimes make spurious moral complaints. Trumping up is a useful tool for grandstanders. By trumping up, grandstanders try to look morally impressive by objecting to features of the world that we moral peasants regard as insignificant, innocent, or even laudable. As moral princesses, they are simply more sensitive about injustice than the rest of us. Notice that, unlike piling on and ramping up, trumping up requires saying something false about morality. You can pile on by repeating an accurate moral assessment, or ramp up by presenting a more radical but true moral view. But to trump up, you must get something wrong.

Trumping up is a regrettably common move in public moral discourse. In 2014, President Obama walked past two Marines and returned their salute while carrying a coffee cup. Normal military protocol recommends against saluting while carrying an object. Conservative commentators rushed to heap moral criticism on Obama. Karl Rove said, "The idea that I'm going to just jaunt out there with my chai tea, and give them the old . . . I mean please, how disrespectful was that?"[19] Breitbart ran a story with the head-line "Obama's Disrespectful 'Latte Salute' Shocks and Offends."[20] It requires a great deal of sensitivity to get as exercised as some did about a minor breach of military protocol. We don't claim to know whether Rove and others were grandstanding, but this moral complaint is certainly trumped up.

Trumping up resembles what philosopher Julia Driver calls moralism, "the illicit use of moral considerations."[21] Moralizing sometimes takes the form of being excessively demanding or strict. You might moralize by claiming, for example, that it is morally obligatory to take the most efficient route possible when driving—no gas-guzzling half-mile detours because the route is more scenic! Other moralizing takes non-moral issues and makes them moral ones. Driver gives the example of an older man who reacts with indignation to an offer lower than the asking price on his home, accusing the prospective buyer of trying to take advantage of the elderly.[22]

Ecologists use the term "invasive species" to refer to species that are not native to an ecosystem but can take hold and dominate within it. Once introduced, they cause instability and damage to other species. The example of kudzu will be familiar to many American readers. A species of vine native to Japan, it was introduced in the American South to combat soil erosion. However, it spread quickly throughout the region, smothering and killing millions of acres of native trees and shrubbery. If you've ever driven through Georgia or the Carolinas, you may have seen hundreds of miles of kudzu lining the interstate. Our tendency to moralize is like kudzu. Once the search for new problems takes hold, it is hard to stop. British philosopher and moral reformer John Stuart Mill observed this tendency in the nineteenth century, writing that "it is not difficult to show, by abundant instances, that to extend the bounds of what may be called moral police, until it encroaches on the most unquestionably legitimate liberty of the individual, is one of the most universal of all human propensities."[23]

Trumping up requires making a mistake about morality. But you need not be grandstanding to say something false about morality. Morality is complicated, and sometimes people make mistakes despite trying their best to get things right. But even if they are trying to get things right, grandstanders are also trying to project an impressive moral image of themselves. Often this goal will conflict with getting things right.

It is easy to see why grandstanding often takes the form of trumping up. Because grandstanders are eager to show that they are morally respectable, they are often *too* eager to identify as moral problems things that others have (correctly) taken to be morally unproblematic. Even if the Recognition Desire sometimes leads people to identify and call attention to genuine moral problems, eventually all the low-hanging fruit will be picked. Legitimate, easy-to-spot cases of wrongdoing will already have been publicized. But the incentive to discover (or invent) new moral charges is ever-present. Thus, some will turn to trumping up.

Grandstanders who trump up moral claims exploit the fact that leveling moral accusations can be a powerful tool for managing others' impression of you.[24] Studies show that public accusations not only decrease others' trust in the accused, they also raise others' trust in the accuser.[25] Making an accusation, particularly about a matter that others have overlooked, signals that the accuser has high moral standards.

Trumping up can be a tricky idea to grasp. Some might worry we are saying any new or unpopular moral claim must be trumped up. But that is not our view at all. We do not deny that moral problems often escape mainstream notice. We need people to alert us to the injustices that others have missed. Views about, for instance, gender and sexuality that are now common were extremely controversial just decades ago. Some moral concerns are both novel and valid.

But there is also false moral innovation and moral entrepreneurship for the sake of recognition. And as we have seen with other forms of grandstanding, trumping up can be difficult, if not impossible, to distinguish from moral talk offered in good faith. If you are concerned with impressing others, there are clear incentives to trump up, and we should expect grandstanders to do exactly that.

STRONG EMOTIONS

In a famous scene from Sidney Lumet's 1976 film *Network*, deranged TV news anchor Howard Beale concludes a rant about moral decay by instructing his viewers to go to their windows and yell "I'm as mad as hell, and I'm not going to take this anymore!" One by one, his viewers poke their heads out of apartment windows and stand on their fire escapes. They scream and vent their anger, excited to hear that their neighbors are just as outraged as they are.

Our technology for displaying anger has improved since then. We don't need to yell out our windows to experience shared outrage. Now virtually everyone, at any time, has a forum to vent their anger. As of March 2018, there are 1.45 billion daily active Facebook users.[26] They post roughly 684,000 pieces of content every minute.[27] There are 330 million monthly active Twitter users.[28] They post about 500 million Tweets each day.[29] Social media platforms make it easy for anyone to express outrage at the latest political dust-up or celebrity gaffe.

But you don't need access to social media to see anger. Turn on cable news or read the opinion section of your local paper. Partisan media in particular is full of people expressing maximum outrage at all hours of the day. For a ten-week period in 2009, political scientist Jeffrey Berry and sociologist Sarah Sobieraj studied American evening cable television news, national talk radio, ideological political blogs, and mainstream newspaper columns from across the political spectrum. They found some form of outrage expressed in 89.6 percent of the hundreds of items in their sample.[30]

When we talk about "outrage," we have in mind a particular kind of anger that involves morality. You can be angry that it rained on your birthday, or that Pluto is not a planet. But we are interested in specifically *moral* outrage. Moral outrage is what you feel when you hear that a child was killed by a drunk driver, or that an apartment building full of civilians was hit in a drone strike.

Sometimes we express moral outrage straightforwardly: "I'm outraged! Obama wore a tan suit to his press conference about the

Islamic State. Does he have no shame? #notmypresident." But outrage can be expressed in many other ways: name-calling, mockery,
insults, emotional displays (such as yelling, screaming, storming
off, blocking on Facebook), obscene language, heated argument,
and wild misrepresentation and exaggeration.[31] If your social media
feeds resemble ours, you've seen them all.

Grandstanding often takes the form of expressions of outrage
and other strong emotions. Expressions of emotion are one more
means of managing others' impressions of what's in your heart. To
see how this works, we need to discuss a bit of psychology.

Over the past decade, psychologist Linda Skitka has explored
what she calls "moral convictions" (sometimes also called "moral
mandates").[32] Think about one of your strongest moral attitudes.
Maybe you think abortion is wrong, or capitalism is evil. Whatever
it is, it's probably one of your moral convictions. These are attitudes
that, in Skitka's words, "seem to be imbued with particular moral
fervor and passion."[33] People often feel either outraged or gleeful
when they talk about their moral convictions.

It's natural to think that if someone gets emotional about something, he probably feels strongly about it. Skitka's work confirms
that suspicion. She found that stronger emotional reactions to various acts or policies (for example, physician-assisted suicide and the
Iraq War) correlated with stronger moral conviction about those
acts or policies.[34] The things you have moral convictions about are
the things you tend to get worked up about.

Skitka's research suggests a display or report of your outrage
about a moral issue can be used to signal the strength of your moral
conviction about it.[35] "Emotion," she tells us, "plays an important
role in informing people about whether their attitudes are moral
convictions."[36] Grandstanders can use these emotional displays
strategically to communicate to others their heightened moral

convictions. Where moral outrage gains social purchase, the implicit assumption is that the most outraged person has the greatest moral insight or the strongest moral conviction about the issue under discussion. Grandstanders exploit this background assumption and employ outrage to signal that they are more affected by moral disorder in the world or empathize more fully with victims of wrongdoing. If lots of things in the world ruffle your feathers, then people will think you must have lots of moral convictions.[37]

To some, this discussion will sound too cynical. They might object that when people express moral outrage, they do so to identify injustice in the world. Outraged people just care about victims of injustice, and their anger leads them to admirable political engagement, peaceful protest, and the punishment of wrongdoers on behalf of those who have no voice or power. Being angry is just evidence that you are paying attention and responding appropriately to the world's problems.

It used to be a common view among psychologists that our motivations for expressing outrage actually were that pure. But in recent years, psychologists Zachary Rothschild and Lucas Keefer have discovered there are other, less admirable motivations behind many expressions of outrage.[38]

One reason people express moral outrage is to alleviate their own guilt.[39] In one study, subjects who felt guilt about using goods made with sweatshop labor reported higher levels of outrage and a greater willingness to punish corporations that run sweatshops than subjects who didn't use sweatshop goods and so felt no guilt. Why did the guilt-ridden sweatshop users report greater outrage? Rothschild and Keefer found that when people feel complicit in moral wrongdoing, they try to alleviate this guilt and protect their images of themselves as good people. They do this by turning to outrage and punitive attitudes toward others. Once expressed, outrage makes them feel morally good once again. Thus, some of the moral outrage you see is probably *defensive*. For example, consider the ongoing calls for awareness of and accountability for sexual assault and harassment prompted by the Me Too movement that began in 2017. One wonders how much of the outrage we see from men in support of this movement is an attempt to assuage guilt over their own transgressions and bolster their self-conceptions as good people.

Moral outrage also makes us feel good. In another study, psychologist Jeffrey Green and colleagues had participants read either a story of injustice (villagers not receiving tsunami aid) or a "neutral" story (shopping for dinner). They found that subjects who experienced a state of righteous anger after reading the injustice story rated themselves as more moral than did those who were in a neutral emotional state after reading the neutral story. Feeling outrage makes us feel like better people. Furthermore, and crucially for our purposes, when given the choice, the people who were angry and had morally self-enhanced after reading the initial story about injustice were more interested in reading *more* stories about injustice than they were in reading "happy" stories that would decrease their anger. Why would they seek out more chances to be angry? The explanation doesn't seem to be that they are trying to alleviate guilt. Instead, they seem to be trying "to buttress their self-conceptions as moral paragons."[40] We apparently enjoy thinking highly of ourselves. One wonders, then, how much anger is an attempt just to keep the moral high going.

If people seek out anger to reinforce their images of themselves as moral paragons, they probably express outrage to get *others* to see them as moral paragons, too. And this has been precisely our claim: that grandstanders use moral outrage to make themselves look like good people.

We have focused on moral anger, but grandstanders could just as easily use other strong emotions to display their moral credentials. Expressions of shock ("I cannot believe that . . . "), disappointment ("I am incredibly disappointed in . . . "), and disgust ("I am absolutely sickened by . . . ") are all promising candidates. Positive emotions work, too. Think of those who report being "so in awe" of someone for his costless stand on some moral issue among like-minded friends.

To be clear, we are not saying that any expression of outrage or other strong emotions is grandstanding. There are many evils in the world, and much of the anger and distress you see is sincere and appropriately directed at serious moral problems. We are also not saying that every time someone has a seemingly misplaced or excessive emotional reaction, he is grandstanding. Sometimes people just get too excited or make honest mistakes. But they also often grandstand. People get outraged for all kinds of reasons, including wanting to impress others with their moral qualities.

DISMISSIVENESS

Grandstanders are frequently dismissive. This is one reason they can be so frustrating and difficult to engage in conversation. It's one thing for someone to think he is better than you. It's quite another to be treated like your moral views and values aren't even worth thinking about. Yet this is precisely the *modus operandi* of many grandstanders. Often, their dismissiveness reveals itself in claims of self-evidence. For example, someone might say:

> "If you cannot see that this war is just, then your views are beneath contempt, and I refuse to engage you any further. And

if you don't understand why, I'm not going to waste my time explaining it to you. Do better."

Grandstanders often talk as if their views are utterly obvious. Anyone competent at making moral judgments would surely come to the same conclusions. This sort of talk can be used to signal that one's moral sensibilities are more finely tuned than those of others, and thus that one is morally respectable. What is not obvious to others is painfully obvious to the grandstander. Moreover, grandstanders often bat away any suggestion of moral complexity, expression of doubt, or disagreement as revealing either an insensitivity to moral concerns or a lack of commitment to morality itself. Indeed, grandstanders often deny that their views need any defense (or they say that were they to give a defense, their audience would not be enlightened enough to understand or appreciate it). Frequently, grandstanders assert their authority to dismiss others by introducing themselves with a credential: "As someone who has long fought against injustice . . . " or "As a patriotic American . . . " Sure, there are some situations in which letting others know you are a physician or lawyer is helpful information. Expertise is relevant. But just as often, introducing yourself "as a . . . " is merely a wind-up for some grandstanding. We are reminded of comedian Demetri Martin's joke that "When someone describes themselves 'as a tax-payer,' they're about to be an asshole."[41]

Of course, some moral and political views are worthier of dismissal than others. We aren't suggesting that whenever someone defends human sacrifice or the Gulags, we must take time out of our day and seriously consider their merits. We also think reasonable people can disagree about which moral claims are obviously true, and which are beyond the pale. But none of this casts suspicion on our claim that people sometimes use dismissive moral talk to assert their moral superiority over others. The danger is that we become so convinced of our own moral righteousness that *any* views that differ from our own become absurd, worthy of ridicule and immediate dismissal. The dark side of moral self-enhancement is that it provides a cover for dismissing almost any view we disagree with.

A FOOLPROOF TEST?

By now you will have noticed that while cases of piling on, ramping up, trumping up, strong emotions, and dismissiveness are sometimes instances of grandstanding, there are also more innocent, well-intentioned instances of each. You might ramp up to try to impress others, but you might also ramp up simply because you disagree with what was just said.

Not everything that looks like one of the categories in this field guide is a case of grandstanding, which is one reason grandstanding can go undetected. It can look or sound just like relatively selfless moral talk. Of course, sometimes the mask does seem to slip. For instance, someone might claim that Donald Trump is the most immoral world leader in the last 100 years. It is plausible that such a person is just trying to show off how much he hates Trump. But in such cases, there are alternative explanations that are also plausible. Some people are just thoroughly ignorant of history. Sometimes people get caught up in the moment and overlook obvious things without at all meaning to seek attention. And onlookers will often lack the information necessary to assess alternative explanations for what someone thinks she's doing.

So while we hope this chapter has helped readers better understand what is going wrong in public discourse, we also want to caution that there is no simple test for identifying grandstanding.

Grandstanding is much like lying. We are all more or less on the same page about what lying is, and have been for a long time, but most people also understand that there is no foolproof—or even very reliable—way to recognize when someone is lying. Despite what you see on television, we don't even do very well at detecting lies with polygraph machines.[42] And law enforcement agents—who receive professional training for detecting lying based on locution, body language, and micro-expressions—barely beat a coin toss in controlled studies.[43]

Similarly, it will be difficult to tell from a single piece of writing or speech whether a person is grandstanding. But contextual clues might help. For instance, you might know that the speaker frequently makes controversial moral claims that he says are obvious to any good person. You might have seen him frequently move to defend the most extreme positions in debates. Or perhaps he tends to insert extraneous information about himself into moral arguments. Knowing someone is a narcissist might clue you in, too.[44] But all this evidence is imperfect and, you must realize, incomplete.

As we will argue in the final chapter, though, it is far less important to identify grandstanding in others than it is to know how to avoid it ourselves.

Chapter 4

The Social Costs of Grandstanding

"Why do we have to fight? . . . Stop hurting America," *Daily Show* host Jon Stewart implored the hosts of *Crossfire*, the CNN debate show known for fiery and unproductive back-and-forths about the controversies of the day. "You're doing theater when you should be doing debate," Stewart continued. "What you do is not honest. What you do is partisan hackery."[1] Stewart's critique, in a nutshell, was that *Crossfire* was giving us all of the costs of political discussion—self-righteous preening, nasty exchanges, and plenty of stretching the truth—with none of the benefits. His now-legendary appearance hit the mark.[2] *Crossfire* was canceled just months later, its credibility shot.

Crossfire had a lot of problems, and we don't want to overstate the comparison between its failings and those of contemporary moral and political talk. The lesson for our purposes is that people expect public discourse to be productive, and when it isn't, they think something has gone wrong. What we want to point out is that grandstanding can play an important role in making public discourse dysfunctional, by introducing costs that don't pay dividends.

By now, you have a sense of what grandstanding is, why people do it, and what it looks like. It is time for us to turn a critical eye to the practice of using moral talk for self-promotion.

We suspect most people find grandstanding annoying. Watching people turn moral discourse into a vanity project makes eyes roll. In this way, grandstanding is like posting too many cat photos on Facebook. Life is full of such minor annoyances, but there is nothing *morally* wrong with them.

But grandstanding is worse than merely being annoying. It is usually morally bad and should generally be avoided, or so we will argue. One of the reasons it's bad is because it has social costs: polarization, cynicism, and outrage exhaustion. We do not mean to suggest, of course, that grandstanding is the only cause of these social costs. But as grandstanding becomes more prevalent in a society's public discourse, there is reason to expect these costs to increase.

POLARIZATION

If you pay much attention to American politics, you have probably heard people say that the current political landscape is "polarized." You may have seen headlines like "America's Political Divide Keeps Getting Wider" (*The Atlantic*) and "Polarization Is Dividing American Society, Not Just Politics" (*The New York Times*).

To polarize something is to divide or split it into two sides. Here's an illustration. To make life difficult for his brother, Brandon recently gave his niece 100 multicolored plastic balls. When she and Brandon toss these balls around, they end up covering the floor in an unstructured mess. But suppose she and Brandon started pushing the balls into two opposite corners of the room. Eventually, the balls would be polarized into two densely packed piles far away from each other.

In recent decades, researchers have found that American voters have become increasingly polarized along moral and political lines in just this way. Liberals and conservatives have been engaged in a process of moving away from each other. This process has resulted in our current state of polarized politics.

Discussion of a few empirical findings can help us see what's been happening. Over the course of the last seventy years, the percentage of people claiming to be either liberal or conservative has consistently risen, while the percentage of people claiming to be ideologically moderate has consistently declined.[3] Political polarization clears out the middle of the political spectrum, just like the balls were cleared from the middle of the room. Furthermore, the policies of the two major political parties have polarized. Democratic policies have moved to the left and Republican policies have moved to the right of the median voter.[4]

Polarization has also affected how we feel about and treat one another. So-called affective polarization refers to the increasing antipathy to those on the "other side." Both Republicans' and Democrats' negative attitudes toward the other party have dramatically increased.[5] According to one recent study, over 40 percent of people from each party now regard the other side as "downright evil."[6] The same study found that 20 percent of Democrats and 16 percent of Republicans report thinking that "we'd be better off as a country" if many members of the opposing party "just died." Perhaps most worryingly, 18 percent of Democrats and 14 percent of Republicans reported feeling that violence would be justified if the other side wins the 2020 presidential election.

Now, we must point out that among political scientists, there is much controversy about the nature and causes of political polarization.[7] Is it caused by social media? Gerrymandering? Is it driven by party elites or the masses? Some researchers even argue that political polarization is largely a myth.[8] These debates are not our focus, but suffice it to say that the majority view among political scientists appears to be that polarization is happening. The political left and right really are "moving apart" from one another in terms of how the electorate self-identifies, the politics of the respective political parties, and how partisans feel about the other side. Indeed, we are now more polarized than we have been in decades.

The causes of polarization are likely numerous and complex, and we aren't proposing a full explanation. But we do think grandstanding contributes to the problem. The use of moral talk for self-promotion causes people to say and believe things that push people further apart.

Social scientists find that when a group of people deliberates about moral or political issues, the group members tend to move toward more extreme viewpoints.[9] This is called "group polarization." The basic idea is that when people get together in a room (or at a bar, or on Facebook, or on cable news "debate" shows) to discuss an issue like abortion or immigration, they will tend to walk away with more extreme views than they had when they started.

Group polarization can happen in two basic ways. The first is a movement of the members of a single group in one direction on an opinion spectrum. Imagine, for example, that after a highly publicized school shooting, a group of people in the community gathers to consider proposing new gun control measures. Suppose that most of the group tentatively supports new measures at the outset. After deliberation, however, the group will tend to move toward enthusiastic support for those same new laws.[10] Call this *intragroup polarization*.

A second kind of polarization involves two separate groups moving further apart from each other, as their individual members are drawn toward more extreme versions of the group's initial view. This might happen when members from both groups move toward extremes, or when only one group does. Imagine two groups of people clashing as they comment on a Facebook post, one generally right-leaning, the other generally left-leaning. After a few rounds of debate, one group coalesces around the view that the only just policy is a federally mandated minimum wage of $25 per hour, whereas the other group ends up supporting the view that all laws regulating wage labor are unjust. In such a case, the polarization occurs in re-sponse to another group's views, which might stay the same or, as in our example, move toward an extreme as well. Call this *inter-group polarization.*

In recent work on group polarization, researchers have found that although group deliberation does sometimes cause individuals to polarize, it does not do this regularly. Instead, deliberation fre-quently results in homogenization—peoples' views end up closer together.[11] So, if group deliberation itself doesn't cause polarization, what does?

Legal scholar Cass Sunstein has suggested one promising ex-planation: people's "desire to maintain their reputation and their self-conception."[12] As we saw in chapter 2, not only do we tend to think highly of ourselves, morally speaking, we want others to think highly of us, too. Sunstein's thought, then, is that members of a group will often want to outdo one another, resulting in increasingly extreme contributions to public moral discourse. They do this to preserve their reputations and self-conceptions as morally impres-sive people. Grandstanding is a mechanism for this preservation. This explains why grandstanding causes polarization when groups deliberate. Polarization is especially likely in cases of ramping up and trumping up, where the competition to out-do others pushes people to adopt more extreme views. A few examples can help illus-trate how this happens.

Let's first think about how grandstanding could cause intra-group polarization. In this case, group members change their views to reaffirm their self-conceptions by expressing stronger views than others in their group. Suppose you are chatting with like-minded progressives, each of whom thinks of herself as caring deeply for the poor. If someone argues that morality demands a $15 per hour minimum wage, why not respond that it is even more caring to institute a $20 per hour minimum wage?

Grandstanding can also cause inter-group polarization as members from both groups change their views to move further from the opposition. Perhaps they will engage in a kind of competition within their own group to see who despises the views of the out-group the most, with the winner holding the strongest contrary view. Naturally, these kinds of competitions could happen in both groups at once.

Suppose we are right that grandstanding is among the causes of group polarization. So what? Why is polarization a bad consequence? We'll have more to say about polarization in chapter 7, where we argue that grandstanding undermines the possibility of compromise. For now, we will argue that grandstanding-driven polarization is dangerous because it leads people to adopt false beliefs, and it makes them overconfident in their beliefs.

False Beliefs

Grandstanding-driven polarization causes people to have false beliefs about the world. You might think this is simply because polarization leads people to hold (or at least say they hold) more extreme and radical views. But this would be a mistake. Extreme or radical views are not necessarily false, after all. Many viewpoints that seem "radical" to us now might actually be true. Furthermore, which viewpoints are considered "extreme" changes over time. In many ways, what is counted as "extreme" or "radical" depends on what is already considered "moderate" or "normal." A hundred years ago, the idea of state-recognized same-sex marriage would have been considered radical by most Westerners, but not so today. So our claim is not that grandstanding leads people to have false beliefs simply because grandstanding pushes them to hold or express radical views.

Rather, grandstanding-driven polarization tends to cause people to have false beliefs because of the incentives built into competitive grandstanding. Recall that much grandstanding-driven polarization typically involves ramping up and trumping up. Notice, however, that ramping up and trumping up are not reliable ways of discovering the truth. What leads grandstanders to alter their views or stated positions is predominantly a desire to hold a prized position within a group. The relevant incentive, then, is not to stop modifying your beliefs or stated positions once you arrive at the truth, or whatever claim is best supported by the evidence. Rather, the incentive is to stop when an even more extreme position would no longer impress the people you want to impress. These incentives will often pull in different directions. Recall our discussion in the previous chapter of how much grandstanding resembles the Cold War arms race. The Soviets and the Americans were not trying to stockpile the objectively correct number of warheads (whatever that might mean). Similarly, grandstanding-driven polarization is unlikely to result in the discovery of the truth about morality and politics.

This might seem obvious, but some examples might help show why grandstanding is not a reliable way of getting at the truth. In an attempt to be seen by their preferred social and political network as being the most opposed to President Trump, many have taken to ramping up or trumping up and, as a result, saying false things. It is not enough to denounce Trump's presidency as terribly incompetent and morally backwards. He must be the worst president ever.[13]

Of course, this phenomenon isn't unique to Trump. Barack Obama was also the worst president ever.[14] So was George W. Bush.[15] And Bill Clinton "may not have been the worst president the republic has had, but he is the worst person ever to have been president."[16]

During discussion of the Republican-proposed Tax Cuts and Job Act of 2017, Congresswoman Nancy Pelosi described the bill on the floor of the House as "the worst bill in the history of the United States Congress."[17] When pressed by a reporter to reconsider her remarks, Pelosi ramped up even further: "No, it is the end of the world. The debate over health care is life and death. This is Armageddon."[18] It is not enough to argue that the tax bill has some good parts and many bad parts, and on balance it is bad. "The bill will lower some peoples' tax burden, but it will also greatly add to the national debt and is too generous with corporations" is too nuanced a position for a purity test. The bill must be disgusting. An atrocity. An abomination! How else will people know how morally serious you are in your opposition? If Pelosi's goal was to communicate her moral purity to partisans, she succeeded. But if her goal was to respond fittingly to a bad bill, Pelosi went too far. Is the GOP tax bill worse than the Alien and Sedition Acts (1798), which criminalized criticism of the U.S. government? Or the Indian Removal Act (1830), which led to the forced removal of Indian tribes from the southern United States? Or the Fugitive Slave Act (1850), which returned slaves that had escaped to free soil back to bondage? Or the Patriot Act (2001), which enhanced state executive power at the expense of civil liberties? That seems rather implausible. As we write this two years after the passage of the tax bill, the world has not ended. You might defend Pelosi by saying she was just being hyperbolic. But that's our point.

Much hyperbole in public discourse is driven by a desire to be seen as having the best moral credentials, at least among your relevant social network. This kind of polarization does not track the truth. Extreme views arrived at via ramping up and trumping up are unlikely to be correct. And if they are correct, it will be a matter of luck, against all odds. In his famous late nineteenth-century work on crowd psychology, French polymath Gustave Le Bon saw why trying impress to others is unlikely to lead to the truth. "A crowd," he wrote "is only impressed by excessive sentiments. . . . To exaggerate, to affirm, to resort to repetition, and never to attempt to prove anything by reasoning are methods of argument well known to speakers at public meetings."[19]

We all pay significant costs when people have false beliefs about matters of morality and politics. This is especially true in democracies, where millions of other people decide who will govern us.[20] Half of Americans endorse at least one conspiracy theory.[21] In 2017, half of Republicans still believed Barack Obama was born in Kenya.[22] Many Americans have false beliefs, not only about the "other side" but also about their own.[23] The average Democrat thinks 44 percent of Republicans earn over $250,000 a year. Republicans themselves estimated the figure to be 33 percent. In truth, only 2 percent of Republicans make that much. The average Republican thinks that 38 percent of Democrats are gay, lesbian, or bisexual. Democrats themselves put the figure at 29 percent. Yet the real number is 6 percent.[24] These kinds of wildly mistaken beliefs are in part due to grandstanding about how the right is full of rich fat cats, and the left is full of people who don't conform to the norms of traditional sexual morality. Grandstanding eventually affects how people come to see not only the other side, but themselves as well.

As legal scholar Ilya Somin concludes from a recent large study, "widespread political ignorance is a serious problem for democracy."[25] How can we expect to deliberate and reflect upon how best to solve the problems facing us if we are so out of touch with reality?

Nor is it easy to correct a false political belief. Studies show it is harder to correct peoples' mistaken beliefs about politics than it is about matters of health.[26] Of course, there are lots of reasons people have false beliefs. But grandstanding-driven polarization is one of them, and we all pay the costs.

Overconfidence

To make matters worse, grandstanding-driven polarization also encourages people to be unduly confident about their views, making those views more resistant to correction.

Suppose you take part in a conversation about gun control, where everyone else supports legislation designed to make guns harder to obtain legally. Let us suppose there is a fair bit of grandstanding going on, with people trying to show how deeply they care about keeping children safe. We predict the group's views will tend to move toward the extreme, with more people defending, for example, a repeal of the 2nd Amendment.

Of course, similar conversations are happening on the other side of the gun issue. Gun advocates tend to move to more extreme positions as well, concluding if we really want to protect students from mass shootings, teachers themselves should be armed.

These kinds of conversations tend to push active participants in public discourse to adopt one of two views: The progressive position that the 2nd Amendment should be repealed, and the conservative position that school teachers should be armed.

Suppose you lean toward the progressive side of matters such as gun control. The fact that the "other side" takes a view so radically different from yours will seem like evidence your side is the reasonable one. If the only viable alternative you see being defended is so extreme, this confirms that *your* view must be the right one.

It's the only acceptable option on the table. To the extent that you fall closer to one extreme than the other, this could lead you to become more confident your view is correct. But of course, to the extent that the polarization you see is grandstanding-driven, you shouldn't be so confident. If both your own view and the opposing view are the result of grandstanding-driven polarization, that's not a reason to be *more* confident you are right. If anything, it is evidence that you should be *less* confident, for the reason we explained earlier: grandstanding-driven polarization leads people to adopt false beliefs.

Studies show that many of us are more confident in our moral and political views than we should be.[27] But when lots of people are unduly confident in their views, this can impose social costs on us all. When overconfident people are wrong, it is more difficult to convince them of that, and they will find it difficult to see weaknesses in their own views. Being overconfident makes it less likely that you will seek out information that disconfirms your beliefs. It will also make you more likely to dismiss opposing views prematurely.

CYNICISM

Think back to when you first started paying attention to public affairs. If you were like us, you started out pretty credulous. You might have taken carefully crafted publicity statements at face value, or believed Bill Clinton when he shook his finger and said he did not have sexual relations with that woman. If you started following the news only recently, you might have seen the Harvey Weinstein statement mentioned in chapter 1 and thought: "Hey, this guy really cares about women." But then imagine learning why he made the statement in the first place. This might be jarring. And then imagine learning that he had donated to and was an outspoken advocate for feminist causes for years. If this were a formative event for you, you'd come to think maybe all his past moral talk was just a cover, or perhaps something he felt he was supposed to do to be lauded as a Respectable Person by the Hollywood elite. Whatever the explanation, it will be hard to resist the inclination to let some cynicism creep in.

Grandstanding breeds cynicism about moral talk. It leads to skepticism and disillusionment about the sincerity of people's contribution to moral discourse. Grandstanding occurs because people want others to think they're on the side of the angels. When observers realize what grandstanders are up to, they begin to think that moral discourse isn't about promoting justice at all. Moral discourse may unfold under the *pretense* of making the world better. But for many, it's all about shoring up your moral credentials.

According to communication researchers Masahiro Yamamoto and Matthew Kushin, "consuming political information on social media increases cynicism and apathy."[28] Certain forms of news media appear to cause cynicism, too. In their book, *The Spiral of Cynicism*, researchers Joseph Cappella and Kathleen Hall Jamieson discovered a positive link between "strategic news" and cynicism about politics and politicians.[29] Much of the news presents politics as a game, with politicians as contestants trying to put on the most appealing act. Consuming that kind of news makes people cynical about the whole idea of politics, precisely because this is the kind of news that contains lots of grandstanding.[30] All the piling on, ramping up, trumping up, displays of strong emotion, and dismissiveness gives you a feeling you can't shake: many people are using moral talk to seem morally superior, increase their social standing within a group, and dominate and silence their supposed moral inferiors.

To be clear, our point is not just that moral hypocrisy (as in the Harvey Weinstein example) leads to cynicism, though that is undoubtedly true. Our point is more nuanced. When people see moral talk used so frequently to impress others—as it is when people grandstand—this gives people good reason to doubt the sincerity of moral talk in general. Why should we take your high-minded moral pronouncements seriously when that kind of talk is usually just personal PR?

Notice that others need not know for certain that people are grandstanding for their cynicism to be reasonable. Yes, individual instances of seemingly obvious grandstanding justifiably make people skeptical about moral talk. But the fact that we know grandstanding is both out there and hard to detect reliably makes us understandably cynical about moral talk in general.

This reaction is at least in part due to a cognitive bias identified by psychologists Justin Kruger and Thomas Gilovich called "naïve cynicism."[31] This is a bias that leads us to expect that others are more egocentrically motivated than they actually are.

Naïve cynicism perhaps has its strongest effects when we are assessing those with whom we disagree. Psychologist Elanor Williams writes that "we may be especially likely to be naively cynical when the other person has a vested interest in the judgment at hand, but if that person is a dispassionate observer, we expect that he or she will see things the way we do (the way things 'really are')."[32] This may explain why you sometimes readily identify grandstanding in certain people, while those with similar beliefs to the apparent grandstander insist they don't see it. We are more likely to think we detect selfish motivations in our political opponents than in those who agree with us.[33]

Why think cynicism about moral talk is bad? Not all cynicism has bad consequences, after all. Cynicism about faith healers and multi-level marketing schemes will spare you some headaches. We are *not* saying that grandstanding is bad because it causes cynicism, and cynicism always has bad results. Rather, our point is that grandstanding-driven cynicism has a uniquely bad effect: it devalues the social currency of moral talk. As a result, moral talk comes to be seen as a nasty business—a battlefield for people trying to prove they are on the right side of history. By debasing moral talk, we render it a less useful tool for accomplishing aims more important than the promotion of reputation. Widespread cynicism about moral talk is a social cost that we all bear simply because some people try to make themselves look good.

We need a way of talking to one another about important moral and political issues. When people raise moral concerns or make moral complaints, we need public discourse to work well enough that people take those concerns seriously. Widespread cynicism ensures that moral talk is more likely to inspire rolled eyes than furrowed brows. And because grandstanding causes cynicism, it undermines the efficacy of moral talk in precisely this way.

We have argued that grandstanding is bad because it makes people more cynical about moral talk. But, someone might object, *this book* will also make people more cynical about moral talk. After all, we are drawing attention to grandstanding and showing how common it is. So won't people be more cynical about moral talk after reading this book? Doesn't it follow that this book is also bad, and writing it was morally wrong? Are we part of the problem we set out to diagnose? Call this the hypocrisy objection: Tosi and Warmke say it's bad to cause cynicism about moral talk, but then why is it okay for them to do it?

There are a few reasons why this objection is not promising. Suppose you think lying is wrong because the more people lie, the more cynical people become about communication. Would it be wrong to report that concern about lying to others? Obviously not. In fact, one of the arguments against lying that nineteenth-century British philosopher John Stuart Mill gives in *Utilitarianism* appeals to the tendency of lying to weaken "the trustworthiness of human assertion."[34] Was Mill a hypocrite? Or consider philosopher Harry Frankfurt's popular essay, "On Bullshit." Frankfurt argues that bullshitting—that is, not caring whether something you say is true or false—interferes with the practice of talking about things that people believe to be true.[35] By explaining what bullshitting is, and showing why it causes cynicism, was Frankfurt a hypocrite? If we're hypocrites, we're in good company.

It might be argued in reply that Mill and Frankfurt's arguments aren't bad in the way that ours is, because everybody already knows about lying, and most people know about bullshitting. But since grandstanding is a relatively little-known idea, our book could potentially do more damage. We doubt that this is true. After bothering most of the people we've met for the past five years about grandstanding, our sense is most people *do* know about it. They also realize it is widespread, and, almost without fail, they go on to mention at least one of their friends' behavior on the internet. What people don't seem as aware of, however, is the fact that so many other people have thought about grandstanding, too.

We are shedding light on the idea of grandstanding, making rigorous moral arguments about it, and letting people know that they are not alone in being bothered by it. We recognize that the concept of grandstanding will be genuinely new to some people, and perhaps they will become more cynical as a result. But that handful of newly cynical people is insignificant compared to the large number of people who have been made into cynics by the widespread phenomenon of grandstanding. If our book has any impact, we expect that the lion's share of it will be in making clear and public what many people are already thinking about grandstanding. And the consequences of that outcome are likely to be far more positive than the mere spread of cynicism.

Now, this could all be true, and we could still be hypocrites. But even so, our arguments may have established a strong moral presumption against grandstanding, which is what they are intended to do. Grandstanding either causes cynicism or it doesn't. We have argued that it does. If you want to challenge that argument, you need to show that grandstanding doesn't cause cynicism. The morality of the authors or this book is another matter, though those topics are of course fair game. The point is just that it's a different issue, unrelated to our argument.

We once heard a story, probably apocryphal, about a philosopher delivering a public talk that was interrupted by a gunman, who took several errant shots at the philosopher. After standing back up from his defensive crouch, the philosopher said, "Even if you had killed me, you wouldn't have refuted any of my arguments." Even if we are hypocrites, that has nothing to do with whether our arguments work.

THE COSTS OF GRANDSTANDING-DRIVEN OUTRAGE

Virtually anyone with internet access has a platform to express anger instantly to hundreds, even thousands of people. By expressing anger in this way, you can communicate something about yourself—you are morally sensitive, you care about injustice—so much so that you're willing to accept the cost of being upset to show it. As we saw in chapter 3, grandstanders know how to use their emotions strategically to display a morally impressive self-image. There are three distinct but related ways that using outrage to grandstand can negatively affect us all.

The Crying Wolf Problem

In some ways, outrage and other strong emotional expressions are good. Expressions of anger can effectively identify bad things in the world and motivate people to address them. But to use outrage effectively, we must protect it. Otherwise, when anger could be used to help people see that something is seriously wrong, displays of outrage will just sound like noise.

Grandstanders don't protect anger. They abuse it. For grandstanders, just about anything can be cause for outrage, from college dining halls serving Chinese food to Obama saluting while holding a coffee cup. Anything can be an occasion to display one's moral purity.

Grandstanding-driven outrage devalues the expression of outrage in general. When outrage is used appropriately, it serves as a red flag that alerts observers that something has gone very wrong. But the indiscriminate use of outrage dilutes its power to identify particularly bad things in the world. When public discourse is flooded with outrage over petty complaints, idiosyncratic moral preferences, and pet causes because someone wants to show off how morally sensitive he is, the meaning of that red flag is devalued.[36]

"It does not have the sting that it used to. For young people, it just doesn't have that much power for them." That's Jesse Sheidlower, lexicographer and former editor-at-large of the *Oxford English Dictionary*, talking, not about outrage, but the word "fuck."[37] The power of the word has been diluted. Why? It's overused. Journalist Joel Achenbach explains:

We must not overharvest the swear words that are part of the commons of our language. It is an adults-only commons, of course. Kids need to be told that they still can't use it. How can a 13-year-old be transgressively vulgar with the word if his 5-year-old sister already uses it? This word is supposed to be a reward of adulthood. We have to conserve it, so that our children and our children's children can use it when we're gone.[38]

You may not think there is much value in conserving the power of the word "fuck." But our point is a more general one: indiscriminate use of a signal can devalue it.

This is the Crying Wolf Problem, named after one of Aesop's most famous fables. A boy tricks his fellow villagers into thinking that a wolf has attacked his flock. They come to help, but there is no wolf. He does this over and over until, when a wolf really does threaten the boy's flock, the villagers ignore him. The wolf devours his sheep.[39] When cries of outrage become commonplace, how can we expect people to identify when danger is truly at the door? When we see someone treat the cultural appropriation of college dining hall food with the same level of outrage she uses in response to police brutality, it is hard to believe her sense of outrage accurately tracks anything important. This person has effectively cried wolf. By contrast, in expressing anger selectively, we protect it as a way to signal significant injustice. If we refrain from using outrage for self-promotion, we reserve its power for more important purposes.

Of course, reasonable people will disagree about what merits outrage. And even when people agree that outrage is merited, they will often disagree about *how much* outrage is appropriate. In other words, we realize that there is a range of appropriate outraged reactions, sometimes including no reaction at all. But we think you'll agree that it would be bad if the signal that outrage sends becomes diluted. Our point is that grandstanding dilutes that signal.

You are faced with a choice, then. You can grab all the attention you can get by grandstanding about how outraged you are. In doing so, you risk rendering your anger ineffective at identifying injustice. Or you can keep your outrage in reserve for when it might actually accomplish some moral good.

Outrage Exhaustion

When public discourse is overrun by constant displays of outrage, people—both contributors and observers of outrage—suffer from *outrage exhaustion*. Outrage exhaustion occurs when people feel outraged too often, or are constantly exposed to it. Consequently, they lose a sense for what is truly outrageous and become unable to muster outrage even when it is appropriate.

We experience emotions at different degrees of intensity. We aren't simply angry or not angry. After an event elicits an emotional response—positive or negative—the strength of that emotion does not remain constant. It fades over time unless more things provoke a similar reaction.[40] When people are repeatedly exposed to triggering stimuli, it reduces the emotional impact of similar stimuli in the future. Psychologists call this habituation.[41] When many of us go through our first break-up, we are likely to sob with Goethe's young Werther that we "have lost the only charm of life."[42] By the end of round twelve, however, it feels more like business as usual.

Because we can be habituated to emotional stimuli, many people who work themselves into constant cycles of outrage end up being less affected by things that used to make them extremely angry. Thus, constant efforts to reinforce outrage are likely to backfire in the long run, as we simply cease to find the latest outrage all that outrageous. The constantly outraged eventually exhaust their capacity to respond with outrage. If you think outrage is an important motivator in times of significant injustice, it is crucial that people be able to retain their capacity for outrage. Grandstanding-driven outrage contributes to unnecessary habituation, thereby causing people to lose a sense for what is truly outrageous.

Here's another way to think about the process leading to outrage exhaustion. Recall that in the previous chapter, we discussed evidence that people seek out moral anger because it makes them feel more virtuous.[43] There is a danger in doing this, though. Namely, as we consume more outrage, it will eventually stop being satisfying. In other words, outrage may follow the law of diminishing marginal utility: the more you get of some good, the less value you derive from an additional unit of that good.[44] For example, if you live in absolute poverty, an extra dollar means a great deal to you. But for Warren Buffett, an extra dollar means almost nothing. Likewise, the second slice of pizza is less desirable to you than the first, the third even less so, and so on. You reach a point of satiation and are indifferent, possibly even averse, to consuming any more pizza. Similarly, when it comes to those who seek outrage to make themselves feel good, outrage is likely to stop being satisfying. The danger, then, is that once we fulfill our craving for moral self-enhancement by using outrage, we won't be as interested in feeling further outrage.[45] And yet, as we have stressed, it is often socially useful to feel and express outrage. Those who have already had their fill of outrage in order to make themselves feel good, however, will have a hard time mustering it when it's needed.

Outrage exhaustion can also prevent us from *acting* on our outrage. In a series of studies, Ernst Fehr and his coauthors have shown that when people witness unfair behavior, they will actually pay to ensure that the wrongdoers are punished—even when they are not the victims of the unfair behavior.[46] The more participants paid, the more their targets were punished. Economists David Dickinson and David Masclet ran an interesting variant on those experiments. In their studies, participants witnessed unfair behavior just like in the Fehr studies. But before they had the option of paying to punish the wrongdoer, they were first given an opportunity to vent their anger.[47] Interestingly, those who vented their anger ended up punishing wrongdoers less than those who didn't vent. They had apparently already gotten some emotional satisfaction through their venting and so didn't have to use punishment to express all their anger. As Dickinson and Masclet point out, there is a bright side to this finding. When punishment is the only outlet for expressing dissatisfaction with others' behavior, we might devote all our energies to punishing and therefore punish more than we should.[48] But there is also a potential downside to venting. If people vent too much through relatively costless expressions of outrage, they might just as easily not do enough by way of punishment. They might even vent so much that they feel comfortable doing nothing else in response to an injustice. Think, for instance, of someone who tweets feverishly about everything scandalous a politician does, but just can't be bothered to volunteer to help people hurt by her policies, canvass for an opposing campaign, or do anything else that would take real effort.

Outrage and other moral emotions are important. What makes these emotions valuable is what they motivate us to do, not just how they make us feel about our moral goodness. But because we can use them to feel good about ourselves, there is a risk that we will not use our outrage well. We will express outrage when we are in the mood to do so, and not when it is appropriate. Outrage is a scarce resource. We should use outrage sparingly, or else it will not be able to do its job when we need it.

One of the most dangerous features of grandstanding is its power to make us feel like we have done something productive when in fact we may have actually done something *destructive* by adding to the pile-ons of the outraged, or exaggerating our beliefs. But there is another extremely insidious effect that we must watch out for. When anger becomes too prevalent in public discourse, even-keeled people will abandon the public square, and many others will be deterred from entering it in the first place.

Moderates Check Out

Many people have little tolerance for constant displays of anger. The whole business is unpleasant, and few of us would ever want to be the target of an online shaming mob. Philosopher Kurt Baier wrote that "moral talk is often rather repugnant. Leveling moral accusations, expressing moral indignation, passing moral judgment, allotting the blame, administering moral reproof, justifying oneself, and, above all, moralizing—who can enjoy such talk?"[49] Baier wrote those words in the 1960s. We can only imagine how he would describe moral talk in popular forums today, but it probably would not be more favorable. Perhaps he would find it encouraging that the general public seems to be coming around to his view about the repugnance of much moral talk. A 2016 Pew Research Center survey found that:

- 37 percent of social media users are "worn out" by the political content they see, and only 20 percent like seeing it.
- 59 percent find it stressful and frustrating to discuss politics on social media with people they disagree with.
- Almost half (49 percent) of social media users find that political conversations they see online are angrier than political

conversations in other areas of life. 53 percent say they are less respectful. 49 percent say they are less civil.

- 39 percent have hidden, blocked, or unfriended someone because of something related to politics.
- 64 percent report that their online encounters with people with opposing political views leave them feeling like they have less in common than they thought.[50]

As we mentioned earlier, many people are being polarized to partisan extremes. Many of the moderates who remain in the middle, however, have had enough of their friends' contributions to public discourse. Indeed, those who are checking out of political discussion are disproportionately moderates.[51] A recent study shows that, by and large, political extremists are the only people who devote much of their social media activity to discussion of politics.[52] Of course, moderates may be exhausted by more than just outrage. Pride, despair, and guilt can also be tiresome, and contribute in their own way to a toxic social environment. Emotionally exhausting discourse turns off many political moderates, who feel unwelcome in a world of polarized groups yelling at each other.

Political scientist Elisabeth Noelle-Neumann's spiral of silence theory of public opinion provides another explanation for why many people avoid moral and political conversations. Most of us fear social isolation. We also know that people who disagree with us or dislike us can orchestrate our social isolation if they please. We've all seen people goad their followers into treating certain unlucky souls as social pariahs simply for making one false move on social media. To encourage the ostracism of those who express socially disapproved ideas is to exert what she calls "isolation pressure."[53] Noelle-Neumann argues that because people fear becoming the target of such campaigns, we choose silence rather than risk exile. Consequently, those who still take their chances in public moral discourse are those with greater confidence that their views will be accepted by those with whom they want to maintain social ties. Such people probably do get acceptance from their inner circle. But they also get a smaller inner circle. Talking morality and politics costs you friends. One study shows that those with more friends are less likely to discuss politics and contested moral issues on social media.[54] Everybody expects the Facebook inquisition.

It is bad for everyone when moderates check out of public moral and political discourse. The most obvious negative effect is that the people who avoid such discussions don't hear arguments and evidence for other views, so their own beliefs go untested. It's easier to maintain your poorly formed convictions if you never discuss them with others, who might show that you're mistaken. But perhaps even worse, when people keep their beliefs to themselves, the rest of the world is deprived of thoughts they otherwise might never encounter. If silent moderates have true beliefs, then other people might never discover the truth themselves. And even if silent moderates are wrong, the reasons they might offer in defense of their beliefs could lead to productive discussions that move others closer to the truth. A healthy public discourse takes all kinds. So when the domain of actively discussed ideas shrinks, we are all worse off for it.[55]

Because moderates check out, political discourse is overrun by activists. Political scientist Diana Mutz has shown that the people most involved in politics are activists at the far ends of the political spectrum. These activists, she also discovered, have the lowest levels of "cross-cutting exposure," meaning they are the least likely to encounter people with political views different from their own.[56] Many activists thus have little idea how people on the other side actually think. Nor do they want to find out. In one study, the majority of people on both sides of the same-sex marriage debate were willing to forgo the chance to win $10 in order to avoid merely being *exposed* to the political views of their opponents.[57]

Of course, not even careful avoidance of moral talk is a guarantee you can stay out of the mess others have made. Some see the world in such thoroughly moralized terms that they expect every person, organization, and product to be sorted into moral and political categories.

Witness the bizarre obsession some have with pressuring pop star Taylor Swift to take a public stance on the presidency of Donald Trump. While many entertainers made their disdain for Trump clear, Swift has (as of this writing) been silent. This has led many to speculate that she is a Trump supporter. Some find in her music a Trumpian ethos: "Swift seems not simply a product of the age of Trump, but a musical envoy for the president's values."[58] Suspicion grew so strong that her lawyer even had to state publicly that she is not a white supremacist. But even if she were to break her silence, this wouldn't please everyone. Broadway actor Todrick Hall astutely observes: "Maybe one day, Taylor will start being super-political, and using her voice to do the things that people think that she should be doing. But even then, she will probably be ridiculed for not being vocal enough, or not being on the right side."[59] In a moral and political climate where you must display your political allegiance, not even a pop star is free to avoid politics and just sing about breakups.

So far, we have argued that there are significant social costs to moral grandstanding: polarization, cynicism, and various bad consequences related to excessive outrage, including the crying wolf problem, outrage exhaustion, and moderates checking out. But just because grandstanding has *some* bad consequences, that doesn't mean that, on balance, it makes the world a worse place. Scolding a child for misbehaving has some bad consequences (she feels sad, you might see some crying), but *overall* the positives may outweigh the negatives. Of course, it's fair to ask whether we're right about which way the scale tips in the final analysis. Are there any possible upsides to grandstanding?

THE SOCIAL BENEFITS OF GRANDSTANDING

While we have focused on the costs of grandstanding, we recognize that it can also produce social benefits. We suspect that, at the end of the day, the costs outweigh the benefits. We haven't argued for that conclusion here; all we have tried to establish in this chapter is a presumption against grandstanding, in light of its significant social costs. Those who want to defend the morality of grandstanding based on its consequences will need to argue either that (1) grandstanding doesn't have the social costs we say it does; or (2) even if grandstanding has those social costs, there are social benefits that outweigh those costs. What might some of those social benefits be?

One potential benefit of grandstanding is that it gives people a chance to signal to others that they are cooperators.[60] This is an important function, because it allows people to build networks of trust that make the gains of social cooperation possible. If someone shows his friends that he's a good person with some well-placed grandstanding, they'll know that they can count on him to keep his word, that he respects other people, and so on. In the same way, grandstanding also pressures others to recognize that they are among people who do the right thing, and so they should follow suit.

There is something to this suggestion. It really is beneficial for all of us that people can signal to one another that they are trustworthy and respectful. But we doubt that this has much to do with grandstanding. Signals are built into everyday behavior, whether we mean to send them or not. You signal to others that you can be trusted by following rules in their presence, like waiting for the walk signal at the crosswalk, not shoplifting from stores, or by refraining from antisocial, self-interested behavior more generally. In other words, we show people that we are cooperators by actually cooperating, not by grandstanding. If people were to stop grandstanding, we would still have ample opportunities to foster social trust through other forms of signaling. In fact, we could do so simply by engaging in moral talk without grandstanding.

In any case, we doubt that grandstanding has much value as a signal of trustworthiness. Other forms of signaling behavior are more reliable because they are harder to fake, and are costlier than simply reciting the right phrases. If anything, grandstanding is more valuable as a tool for manipulation than a signal that the grandstander can be trusted. We refer you again to the example of Harvey Weinstein's apology letter, as well as other cases of grandstanding male feminists who turned out to be sexual harassers and abusers. That grandstanding can be used as cover for bad behavior in this way could lead people to be more cynical about the signals that moral talk actually sends. Our skepticism notwithstanding, we think this issue merits further exploration.

Another strategy for identifying the social benefits of grandstanding is to point to the positive things grandstanding can lead people to do. Consider, for example, the phenomenon of "rage-giving": donating to a political cause or charity out of outrage. Elizabeth Dale, an expert on philanthropy, explains:

> Donating is more than just being outraged on social media, or among friends and family. It is tangible, it's something that people

can do, often without much personal cost to themselves. There is a psychological effect to charitable giving—the idea that I can do something, even if it's contributing a $50 or $100 gift—that can alleviate feelings of guilt, or demonstrate a person's morals and values. By giving on Facebook or sharing that you made a gift on social media, we demonstrate our values to others.[61]

When enough people get outraged about some event, they can channel their anger into productive action. Take, for example, the public outcry over the Trump administration's "zero tolerance" policy on illegal immigration, which led to greater incidents of family separation. By tapping into the collective outrage, a Silicon Valley couple raised $20 million to help reunite children and their families at the U.S.-Mexico border.[62]

Whether you agree with the organizers of this fundraiser about immigration policy or not, the point is that lots of anger expressed on social media—some of it surely grandstanding-driven—can lead people to donate to a charity they believe in. That can be a great result. Of course, you don't have to be grandstanding to express outrage or publicly support political causes. So this is not necessarily a defense of grandstanding, but of outrage speech that motivates charitable giving, and we haven't argued against that. We haven't even argued against the use of outrage. In fact, we claimed that outrage has a place and serves an important good. But that's precisely why we should protect it—so it can be used for truly important causes, not petty moral concerns selected just to demonstrate moral sensitivity.

Here again, our skepticism notwithstanding, we think this a worthwhile avenue to explore. The main challenge will be to produce evidence that grandstanding has a unique social benefit that cannot be attained as easily through moral talk that isn't motivated by the Recognition Desire.

However, even if critics could show that the social benefits from moral grandstanding outweigh its costs, we still have other arguments against grandstanding, independent of its social costs, to unfold in the coming chapters. For example, as we'll see next, grandstanding is morally problematic because it involves disrespecting others.

Chapter 5

Grandstanding and Respect

Everyone deserves to be treated with respect. Some would say ensuring respect for others is the whole point of morality. Why is assault morally wrong? Because it's a failure to treat others with the respect they deserve. Why is racial discrimination morally wrong? Because it's a way of failing to treat people with equal respect.

Moral talk is one of our most useful tools for seeing to it that people are treated with respect. Moral talk is how we communicate that people aren't being treated right. For example, suppose you tell others: "This immigration policy is unfair to children." Your goal is to get people to notice that people aren't being treated with sufficient respect.

The point is that moral talk is a tool. It allows us to work together to make sure people are treated with respect. But like many tools, moral talk can be put to alternative uses. Some of these uses are less than admirable.

Consider the hammer. Hammers can be used to build homes. But they can also be used to hit people. Whether swinging a hammer is a good thing depends on what it's being swung at and why. Like hammers, moral talk can be put to good use. But moral talk is not magic. It can also be used in ways that *disrespect* others.

In this chapter, we argue that grandstanders use moral talk in ways that mistreat others. The claim is not that grandstanding is wrong because it has bad consequences, as we argued in the last chapter. Instead, we'll show that grandstanders fail to treat others with respect.

In certain cases, grandstanding disrespects people. It does this either by using others to show how good the grandstander is, or by misleading others about how good the grandstander is. Then we'll argue that, more generally, grandstanding takes advantage of others by free-riding on their conscientious use of moral talk.

SHOWCASING

If you've watched enough television, you will have encountered the trope of the character facing an impending prison sentence who is advised to find the biggest, toughest looking inmate on his first day inside and pick a fight with him. The idea is to send a message to the rest of the prison population that the new guy will not tolerate any abuse from even the most imposing prisoner, and so he should not be messed with. While we doubt the effectiveness of this strategy in the prison context, the aggressive impulse to harm another person simply to demonstrate something about oneself to onlookers is quite common. Sadly, people are often prepared to take advantage of others to make themselves look good.

Some grandstanders take this approach to public discourse. They go through life looking for opportunities to pounce on others' moral mistakes, real or imagined, to demonstrate to others what good people they are. We call this kind of demonstration *showcasing*. Showcasing involves using others by recruiting them into a public display designed to show off the moral qualities of the grandstander. Showcasers might do this by piling on in cases of public shaming, ramping up or trumping up accusations of wrongdoing, or engaging in accusatory expressions of outrage or other negative emotions. Showcasers are grandstanders who satisfy their Recognition Desire by using the alleged moral failures of others to show off their own moral superiority.

What is wrong with showcasing? Let's take the easy case first: when the showcaser pounces on an *innocent* person to impress others with her moral greatness. Here, the showcaser has clearly done something wrong. It is disrespectful to publicly blame people for things they didn't do. They don't deserve to be treated that way. Just like it would be wrong for the state to put innocent people in jail to show that it cares about justice, it is wrong for grandstanders to shame, ostracize, and embarrass innocent people to show that their hearts are in the right place.

But what's wrong with showcasing if the target is guilty? You might think there is nothing wrong with using blame and shame to display your moral credentials if the target has done wrong. Let's call this the Dirty Harry Defense of showcasing. In the 1973 film *Magnum Force*, Clint Eastwood's character, Inspector "Dirty" Harry Callahan, is assigned the task of tracking down a dangerous killer. Harry requests two sharp-shooting rookie cops as backup. His Lieutenant bristles at the idea of sending two rookies on such an important assignment. "Suppose they panic and start shooting?" the Lieutenant asked. "Nothing wrong with shooting," Harry replies, "as long as the right people get shot."

A defender of showcasing might reason similarly: it doesn't matter why people publicly shame their targets if the targets deserve it. Sure, it's disrespectful to showcase when using innocent people. But this doesn't mean it's disrespectful when you target wrongdoers.

There is a nugget of truth in this defense of showcasing. If a wrongdoer responded to a grandstander's blame by accusing the grandstander of using him to look good, it would be fair to say the wrongdoer was engaging in misdirection. After all, the grandstander's self-interested motivations don't change the fact that the wrongdoer is guilty. But there are good moral objections to showcasing, even when the target has done wrong.

Notice that the Dirty Harry Defense only works if a showcaser has correctly identified wrongdoers for use as instruments of self-promotion. But how successful will showcasers be at targeting only the guilty? We often blame the innocent even when correctly identifying wrongdoing is our *only* goal. When we mix in other, more self-serving motives, how accurate will we be at blaming only the guilty?

You might think showcasers will be accurate in picking only on wrongdoers, because it is only in those cases that their showcasing will be effective. After all, who would think of you as a moral paragon if you pounce on people for doing morally innocent things like painting in their free time, or taking their kids to the park? Perhaps showcasers will only pick on guilty people, because only then will others be impressed.

But this expectation is too optimistic. Recall that many grandstanders try to impress their in-groups. They want their like-minded friends to think of them as being extremely sensitive to injustice, for example. But although it might be difficult for some to accept, our in-groups do not always respond appropriately to moral problems. Even if we assume our group has all the right values, that hardly guarantees that the group will make the correct moral assessment of a person's behavior in a particular case. Life is complicated, and even tightly-knit groups of people with a common moral perspective are bound to encounter new combinations of circumstances that pit some of the group's own values against each other. It would take a true fanatic to believe that her in-group (or even any one member of it) will always arrive at the morally correct answer, no matter what the world throws its way. After all, how likely is it that although everyone else throughout history has had mistaken moral beliefs, you and your group have suddenly become infallible at discovering the moral truth?

We must also keep in mind what we know about the psychology of group dynamics. People often feel pressure to conform their public judgments to what they think others expect of them. Since groups are bound to make faulty moral assessments, individuals trying to impress their groups will often end up using innocent people for showcasing.

Our point is that when we try to impress our in-groups by showcasing, we will often blame and shame innocent people, whether we believe this is what we are doing or not. Knowing we are prone to this error should lead us to lower our confidence that any given case of showcasing targets a wrongdoer. In many cases, we should not be confident at all.

Is it respectful to blame and shame people to make yourself look good if you are likely to pick innocent targets by mistake? Consider an analogous case. Suppose you're a police officer on highway patrol. You haven't had your radar gun calibrated in weeks, and you know there's only around a 60 percent chance it provides accurate readings. But you're close to setting a monthly record for tickets issued, which would impress your Sergeant, and your annual performance review is coming up. You don't want to waste time calibrating when you could be issuing more tickets. Does issuing tickets to drivers using such an unreliable instrument strike you as disrespectful? If so, you should think that much showcasing will be disrespectful too, for the same reason.

But what about showcasing when you are justifiably confident that your target is guilty? There are plenty of cases of clear wrongdoing from celebrities or politicians. Why would showcasing in these cases be disrespectful? In these cases, too, showcasing can go awry.

To see this, notice that even if a showcaser's target is guilty, this does not mean that her desire to impress others will lead her to blame and shame the wrongdoer appropriately. It is possible to treat wrongdoers more harshly than they deserve. Due to the incentives built into social comparison we discussed in chapter 2, much showcasing, like grandstanding in general, will involve ramping up and trumping up. These incentives lead showcasers to be disproportionately harsh in their treatment of wrongdoers.

Nowhere is this clearer than in cases of online shaming.[1] One Twitter user notes, "It's weird I can type something in this box that will destroy my life."[2] It is *de rigueur* for members of the social media mob to send death threats, harass the wrongdoer's family and friends, and lobby the wrongdoer's employer to fire her. For those who think of moral talk as magic, all of this is just another day at the office. Sure, they may be contributing to a cascade of internet shaming, but sometimes justice demands sacrifice—of others, naturally.

Journalist Jon Ronson details the case of Lindsey Stone, who became a victim of online shaming after posting to Facebook an edgy photo of herself making a lewd gesture at a sign requesting silence and respect at Arlington National Cemetery. After going through the usual ordeal of losing her job and getting death threats, Stone was left depressed and unemployable, since any internet search would instantly recall the details of her mistake, complete with photographic evidence. She resumed something resembling a normal life only after Ronson secured for her the *pro bono* services of a reputation management firm, which manipulated search engine results to push links to news of the incident down in the search rankings.

This process requires constant maintenance of a curated on-line presence, complete with fake innocuous public journal entries about trips to amusement parks to clog up the first page of Google search results. According to the reputation management company's estimate, scrubbing Stone's online reputation required hundreds of thousands of dollars' worth of services.[3] We linger over these details to highlight how costly a minimal uptick (if any) in reputation for showcasers can be for their targets. That there is a whole industry devoted to addressing this issue shows that something has gone very wrong in the way we practice moral blame. The details of cases like Stone's are difficult to stomach, and they make it abundantly clear that her tormenters have done something despicable.

Even if Stone acted wrongly, the response she suffered was disproportionate. Surely she didn't deserve death threats. But what about cases where you know for certain that the target is guilty, and your blame and shame are exactly what she deserves? Even here, showcasing can go awry. Coordinating group activity is difficult. Even if the target deserves *your* blame and shame, that doesn't mean she also deserves similar blame and shame from 10,000 other people. Much showcasing takes the form of piling on. Here, individual group members pile their blame and shame onto a wrongdoer, each person putting his two cents in until the total effect of their harassment is orders of magnitude greater than what the wrongdoer deserves.[4] At the very least, your individual status-seeking contributes to group behavior that is disrespectful, even to a wrongdoer.

In an interesting twist, massive online blaming and shaming campaigns sometimes backfire. Psychologists Takuya Sawaoka and Benoît Monin conducted four studies showing that expressions of outrage against racist, unpatriotic, or sexist online posts are seen as less praiseworthy when they are part of a larger group pile-on.[5]

Further, Sawaoka and Monin show that viral outrage triggers a sympathetic response to the offender from observers. This presents a puzzle for showcasers. Even if their shaming might look appropriate in isolation, showcasers who pile on can induce sympathy for their target and make the showcasers themselves look bad.

But the wrongness of showcasing arguably doesn't depend on disproportionate blame or social sanctions. Even if a wrongdoer deserves to be blamed, it is still possible to act wrongly in blaming that person. To see how this is possible, imagine that Ann sees Ben commit some minor moral wrong. It would not be wrong for Ann to call Ben to account for his actions in front of other people. Perhaps it is even the right thing to do, and so she does so. But suppose Ann is in a terrible mood, and is eager to let loose on someone. Even though it was not out of bounds for Ann to call Ben to account, her motivation for calling him out is faulty. Ann doesn't care who she lashes out at, or why. If Ben hadn't come along, she would have taken her bad mood out on someone else instead. Ann treats Ben as an interchangeable punching bag. But that's not what morality is for. Ben should be blamed for his behavior because he did something wrong, not because blaming him makes Ann feel good.

We can use this case to illustrate why showcasing is wrong for the same reason. Suppose that instead of being in a bad mood, Ann felt like her virtue was underappreciated. When Ben slips up, she sees her opportunity, and broadcasts her superior moral qualities to everyone in earshot by tearing into Ben. Here too, Ann acts wrongly in blaming Ben just to show off her moral credentials.

You might object that in both versions of the case, Ann did nothing wrong. Why? Because in fact she punished a guilty person. Because Ben was guilty in both cases, she had a right to punish him. Thus, there was nothing wrong with doing so.[6] Sure, she was fully prepared to lash out at anyone to get what she wanted, but fortune smiled upon her and sent her a guilt-free opportunity to vent her spleen.

It's true that Ann's behavior is less bad when her target is guilty Ben, rather than some innocent bystander. But it is a mistake to ignore her attitude toward other people in the evaluation of her behavior.[7] She simply got lucky that she took advantage of a guilty person. Again, morality is not a convenient excuse to use another person. Morality requires us to treat other people according to their worth as human beings, not as mere instruments. Showcasing fails to do so.

DECEIT

Throughout the book, we have found it useful to compare grandstanding with lying. For example, lying and grandstanding are both ways of doing something morally wrong through your communication. Also, as with lying, it is usually hard to know whether someone is grandstanding just by examining their words. By pointing out its similarities to the more familiar idea of lying, we hope to make it easier to understand grandstanding. We will now argue that some instances of grandstanding have still more in common with lying.

We think grandstanders are usually sincere—they believe the things they say, or they are reporting their actual moral beliefs to others. We have argued that grandstanding is wrong for many other reasons that do not require insincerity (and there are still more arguments to come). But grandstanding can also be wrong because, like lying, it deceives others.

Let's focus just on lying for a moment. Lying is an attempt to deceive another person into believing something the liar himself believes to be false.[8] One plausible explanation for why lying is typically wrong is that by deceiving another person, you fail to treat her with the respect befitting a moral equal. Suppose a friend of yours wants to be a barber. You would never let her cut your hair, but you want to support your friend, so you tell a coworker she's an excellent and experienced barber. You know the truth and make use of it by not letting her cut your hair. Because you lied to your coworker, on the other hand, he has bad information. As a result, he does something he otherwise wouldn't have done. By lying to him, you have treated his practical interests as less important than your own. You have exploited his trust and manipulated him into serving your goal of supporting your friend. In short, you have taken advantage of him by lying to him.

It is also possible to deceive, manipulate, and take advantage of others by grandstanding. Grandstanders sometimes do this by cultivating impressions of themselves as trustworthy, and then exploiting the trust they inspire—whether they mean to do so or not. Grandstanders often seek to establish reputations as being above reproach, or perhaps as merely decent people. But the truth of the matter may be far from the sterling image grandstanders project.

Some grandstanding is unintentionally deceptive. As we saw in chapter 2, there's a good chance you aren't as morally good as you think you are. People overwhelmingly rate themselves as morally better than average. They cannot all be right. Many people really are mistaken about how they compare with others when it comes to their moral qualities. So if you are trying to get people to think of you as morally exceptional, you are probably deceiving them—your grandstanding is aimed at getting people to believe things about you that are actually false. Even if you are not trying to deceive others, you might be doing so all the same.

You might insist that *you* wouldn't make this mistake. Perhaps not. But psychological research gives us good reason to think we are poor judges of our own moral qualities. The "better than myself effect" provides particularly striking reason to doubt ourselves. In one study, participants were asked to estimate what percentage of the time they would exhibit certain traits, such as cooperativeness, honesty, politeness, and trustworthiness.[9] In total, they rated themselves on twenty-six traits. Weeks later the same participants were reassessed. The experimenters told them that they would be presented with the average self-ratings from their peers on each trait. They were then asked to rate themselves in comparison with the average. Across twenty-three of twenty-six traits, the participants rated themselves considerably better than average. The biggest differences were in their evaluations of the four moral traits: cooperativeness, honesty, politeness, and trustworthiness. What's interesting to note is that when participants were asked how they compared to the "average," they were actually given their *own* previous self-ratings. In effect, when they said they were better than average, they were claiming they were better than themselves. This suggests we are not reliable judges of how good we are—whether in absolute terms, or relative to others. So while it is true that some people will be better than average, perhaps you should not be confident that *you* are better than average. Odds are, if you are projecting an image of yourself as a moral saint, you are being deceptive.

Of course, in these cases we have stipulated that you are not trying to deceive others. You sincerely believe you are morally great and want others to think so, too. But that doesn't mean your grandstanding can't be deceptive. It just means your deception isn't intentional. Even if deceptive grandstanding isn't intentional, it may still be irresponsible. When you grandstand, you do something that runs a high risk of deceiving people. After all, what are the odds that you are as morally great as you think you are? Probably not very good. When it comes to misleading others, grandstanding is risky behavior. Since it is wrong to mislead people for personal gain, we would treat others more respectfully if we didn't grandstand.

On the other hand, some grandstanding *is* intentionally deceptive. In these cases, grandstanders don't think they are as morally great as their grandstanding would suggest, but they want others to believe they are anyway. This kind of grandstanding is much like lying, in that it aims at deceiving others. Again, it is generally wrong to deceive others. Insofar as such grandstanding would be aimed at deceiving others, it too would be morally wrong.

You might think that even if grandstanding is often deceptive, it is not a significant moral wrong. We all puff ourselves up a little bit for others, making ourselves look funnier, more attractive, or smarter than we truly are. It is pitiable that some people go to great lengths to convince others that they are smarter, stronger, or more romantically accomplished than they actually are. But outside of extreme cases, those who are successful in these efforts are unlikely to do much damage as a result.

Grandstanding is worse than these other cases, though. The inaccurate perception that grandstanders create in others enables them to take advantage of people in ways that go beyond mere deception. By presenting themselves as better people than they really are, many grandstanders garner others' trust in a way that is not deserved. Grandstanders can exploit this trust in a host of ways.

For example, some people use their grandstanding as a cover for their own bad behavior. Psychologist Anna Merritt and colleagues conducted a series of experiments showing that people seek moral credentials when they fear that their future behavior could appear immoral.[10] In one study, participants were told they were making a hiring decision, and they would have to choose between a white and a black candidate. Some participants were shown descriptions of qualifications where the black candidate was stronger than the white candidate, and others saw the reverse. Before making the hiring decision, participants took a questionnaire asking whether various kinds of behavior were racist. Participants were told that their answers to this questionnaire would be shown to their peers, along with their hiring decision. The researchers found that participants who were shown the files in which the white candidate was better qualified were more likely to criticize behavior as racist in the questionnaire. By preemptively displaying their heightened sensitivity to racism, subjects apparently hoped these credentials would allow them to escape criticism for favoring a white candidate over a black candidate.

This sort of preemptive signaling isn't always morally wrong, of course. Sometimes we need to go out of our way to show that our behavior is morally permissible when first appearances suggest otherwise. Our point is simply that these same motivations are at play when particularly bad people use their grandstanding to make it easier to take advantage of others' trust. By grandstanding, people can build up their moral reputation to avoid suspicion and perhaps even escape criticism when their misdeeds are discovered.

People can also use the trust they secure by grandstanding to ensnare victims. Going further, they can use this trust to discourage their victims from coming forward by preemptively sowing seeds of doubt about the plausibility of their accusations. The fact that grandstanding makes it easier to abuse others is what separates it from other kinds of enhanced self-presentation that are morally innocent. Some examples will help demonstrate what we mean.

Recall the letter Harvey Weinstein released in response to the sexual misconduct allegations against him. By stressing his support for progressive political causes and his profound respect for women, Weinstein attempted to fall back on the reputation he cultivated through years of deceitful impression management, and to buy leniency by dangling the possibility of future good works that would be impossible if he were held responsible for his actions. Besides the transparency of his motives revealed in the letter itself, the fact that he was attempting to manipulate his audience to buy himself greater liberties is further confirmed by the fact that he apparently said similar things when confronted privately, well over a decade before the more recent allegations.[11]

In ostentatiously presenting himself as politically progressive throughout his career, Weinstein made it less likely that accusations against him would be believed, and by extension less likely any of his victims would come forward. His grandstanding has stopped working (for now, at least), but he was able to use it along with his professional power to engage in terrible abuse for years. In short, Weinstein's grandstanding induced people to trust him far more than he deserved.

Some grandstanders probably manipulate people without even realizing they are doing so, and perhaps end up deceiving themselves in the process. Consider the case of Ted Haggard, the former pastor of New Life Church, a megachurch located in Colorado Springs, Colorado. Haggard was also at one time the president of the National Association of Evangelicals, an association of tens of thousands of theologically conservative churches representing millions of members. Haggard rose to national prominence in the mid-2000s in part due to an appearance in a television documentary, *The Root of All Evil?* There he reacted angrily to interviewer Richard Dawkins's questions about science and evolution, decried his arrogance, and ordered him to leave. Haggard's treatment of Dawkins was a clear display of self-righteous anger, directed at an out-group member whose vices he was unwilling to tolerate.[12]

Haggard also attracted media coverage for his outspoken support of an amendment to Colorado's constitution that would ban state recognition of gay marriages. He dismissed the idea that the issue even merited serious discussion, saying, "We don't have to debate about what we should think about homosexual activity. It's written in the Bible."[13] Thus, Haggard demonstrated to all those listening that the answer to what was then a hotly contested issue was simple and obvious to him. Soon after these events, Haggard was publicly accused of carrying on a years-long affair with a male prostitute from whom he purchased crystal methamphetamine. Although he disputed the charges at first, Haggard later admitted that they were true.

Because of his public displays of moral purity, Haggard's congregation likely trusted him all the more. But he might also have succeeded in deceiving himself about his own integrity. As we saw in chapter 3, people sometimes manipulate their own moral emotions, such as anger, to enhance and maintain their impressions of themselves as morally good.[14] Much of Haggard's public outrage and grandstanding may have functioned in large part to convince *himself* that he was actually a good person, despite his failure to live up to his own standards of sexual morality. Through his grandstanding, Haggard deceived his congregation, and maybe himself, too.

There is a practical lesson to be drawn from cases like Haggard's. We know that most humans think better of their moral qualities than is warranted. So we should be wary of the temptation to grandstand to feel better about ourselves. If we do so, we risk feeding into our own delusions, and drifting further and further from an accurate impression of who we are and what we care about.

It might be objected that our worries about deception are overblown. People are not stupid. They know that everyone wants others to think well of them, and so we all expect people to fudge a bit in what they show of themselves to the world. Since we are so aware, we will discount accordingly when we see self-inflation in the form of moral grandstanding, and thereby avoid being deceived.

The trouble with this objection is that grandstanding is generally not direct enough to be detected easily. Otherwise, it wouldn't be effective. The ability to impress others by grandstanding is a skill people possess to varying degrees, as is the ability to see through a deceptive self-presentation. When people say what we want to hear on moral and political matters, we are liable to be taken in by an effective grandstander. It would be awfully naïve to say about deception of this kind or any other that we can just see it and easily discount it.

We're able to see through the Weinsteins and the Haggards of the world, at least after the fact. We know the people involved are grandstanding, and we can adjust our level of trust in them accordingly. But we do not always have this ability. It is alarming to think about how many people are widely trusted or even beloved simply because they are gifted grandstanders. If we respect other people, we won't grandstand to make them trust us more than they otherwise would.

So far, we have given two arguments for the conclusion that grandstanding is wrong because it is disrespectful. First, when grandstanders showcase—that is, blame and shame others to show off how good they are—they treat people as interchangeably useful punching bags. Second, when grandstanders deceive others about how morally good they are, not only is this itself usually disrespectful, but by gaining the undeserved trust of others through deceit, grandstanders are able to abuse others and get away with wrongdoing more easily.

Notice that these arguments were aimed specifically at cases of grandstanding that involve showcasing and deceit. But you can grandstand without showcasing or deceiving others. So we don't think that these arguments show that all cases of grandstanding are disrespectful. Just many of them.

FREE-RIDING

One of the great advantages of life in a stable society is that we get to enjoy the fruits of cooperation with others on large-scale projects. Everyone does his or her part, however small, and follows the rules. The result is a significant common benefit. For example, many cultures have a general practice of standing in line for service. The usual rule is that people allow those who arrived before them to be served before they seek service themselves. As a result, what could be a disorderly and conflict-ridden process is (usually) simple and peaceful.

As cooperative projects grow in size, however, difficulties emerge. One problem is that some people can take advantage of others' good-faith contributions. These people defect from the cooperative rules governing interaction to get greater benefits for themselves. This "free-riding" disrespects those who follow the rules. In this section, we will suggest that our practice of public moral discourse is one such large-scale cooperative practice. We argue that grandstanders free-ride on others' good behavior in public discourse. This is another way grandstanders disrespect others.

Suppose there is a large, grassy pasture. You and nine neighbors let your cows graze in the pasture. The pasture has a carrying capacity of 100 cows. This means that if no more than 100 cows graze on the land, there will be plenty of grass for future cows to eat. If more than 100 cows are allowed to graze, however, the pasture will be ruined from overgrazing.

At first, each neighbor lets only two cows graze in the pasture. But then one of your neighbors realizes that if he lets a few more cows graze, he can make more money. After all, twenty grazing cows are well below the carrying capacity of the pasture. Even with a few more cows grazing, there will still be plenty of grass to go around.

Other neighbors notice this strategy, and they too let more of their cows graze. You realize that if you don't let more of your cows graze, too, you lose out.

What is likely to happen as people continue to add cows, and the pasture nears its carrying capacity? You could stop adding more cows yourself, but why would you? You have no assurance that your neighbors will respect the limit, and it would be too much work to monitor the pasture around the clock to ensure it isn't overgrazed. Why be the only sucker who doesn't take what he can get while the pasture is still there?

It is in the collective interest of everyone to preserve the pasture so it can continue to be of use. But when people act out of narrow self-interest in an unregulated common space with scarce resources, you have the ingredients for the destruction of the pasture. This type of scenario is known as a tragedy of the commons.[15] We can all see such tragedies coming, but if we can only choose what to do for ourselves, we cannot prevent them. The best we can do as individuals is to try to grab what we can of the common resource before it is wiped out.

Our practice of moral talk is, in a way, a common resource like the pasture. Moral talk is a valuable resource. As we explained in chapter 1, moral talk is our primary means of bringing morality to bear on practical problems. We solve, or at least attempt to solve, many important problems using this resource. But much like the pasture in the story can be overgrazed, moral talk can also be destroyed through abuse. We abuse the common resource of moral talk when we moralize excessively, make plainly false or absurd moral claims, or use moral talk in nakedly self-serving ways. These are all things that happen when people engage in moral grandstanding, and, as we have argued in the previous chapter, they result in a degradation of the social currency of moral talk.

What can we do in the face of this problem? Like cattle herders, we could shrug our shoulders and take what we can for ourselves while there are still rubes who take moral talk seriously. But cattle herders have another option, and so do we: mutual submission to a set of rules or norms that protect the common resource.

In the case of the pasture, a system of rules about property would keep the herders from ruining it. Rather than engage in costly monitoring of one another's grazing practices, the herders would do best to become responsible for their own section of the pasture, and so gain both an interest in preserving that section and an ability to exclude others from ruining it.

It doesn't make sense to privatize moral talk, of course. Communication by its nature relies on shared resources. But thankfully there are other ways to prevent a tragedy of the commons.[16] One such solution involves adopting norms that protect the practice of moral talk from abuse. When enough people adopt the norms (and are punished for violating them), we can prevent the degradation of moral talk.

To see what we mean, consider philosopher H. P. Grice's thought that conversations can be cooperatively useful only if those involved follow certain general principles.[17] He called these conversational maxims. Examples of such maxims include "Do not say that for which you lack adequate evidence," "Be relevant," "Avoid obscurity of expression," and "Be orderly." These are general principles we all should follow in general conversation. If enough people stopped following these norms, conversation would be pointless as a cooperative venture. We'd ask if you liked tea and you'd answer, "I love sailing." (A violation of the "be relevant" norm.) Conversation works because we all follow some general rules.

We think there are also norms that govern profitable moral talk, which is one reason why most people find grandstanding so annoying. We all know you can make yourself look good by taking a public stand for what is right. We also all know that making yourself look good is not the point of taking a stand. Consider the cliché of the publicity-hungry politician who transparently uses moral talk about political causes to self-promote. Someone who uses moral talk that way is violating the norms of acceptable social behavior. We suggest a maxim for moral conversation: "Do not use moral talk to self-promote." If enough of us follow this general rule, we will protect the resource of moral talk.

Suppose we are right that this is a good norm of moral conversation. Then it would be wrong to grandstand because it is unfair to everyone else who preserves the profitability of moral talk by refraining from grandstanding.[18] Non-grandstanders could use moral talk to make themselves look good, and they could probably even get away with it much of the time. But instead they restrain themselves and follow the norms that direct them to use moral talk for the sake of promoting justice in the world. Because enough people exercise self-restraint, we all get to enjoy the benefits of living in a society where moral talk is effective. Grandstanders, on the other hand, have it both ways. They enjoy the benefits of everyone else's self-restraint and still use moral talk to improve their social status. In other words, they free-ride on everyone else's sacrifices while refusing to sacrifice in the same way. They take advantage of others, and act as if they are entitled to greater freedom than the rest of us.

Some readers will notice an affinity between this argument and the ones made in the previous chapter about the bad consequences of grandstanding. Indeed, one worry about free-riding is that it could lead to a reduction in the benefits of cooperation, or even the failure of the whole system of cooperation. But it is important to see that free-riding is wrong even if no one suffers any tangible harms because of it. Free-riding is wrong because it is unfair, regardless of what else it causes. When people cooperate under a set of rules, they owe it to one another to follow those rules. When someone breaks a rule, she fails to respect her fellow cooperators as equals. That, and nothing else, is the source of the wrong in free-riding.

Someone might agree that moral talk is helpfully understood as a cooperative practice, but insist we are mistaken about its norms in an important way. Perhaps the primary point of morality, according to some evolutionary theorists, is to enable cooperation among people who regard themselves as bound by their commitments. Moral talk enables cooperation between such people by allowing them to signal to one another that they are trustworthy, particularly by blaming or punishing wrongdoers.[19] Thus, signaling to others about your moral qualities might be more important than our view seems to allow, and it should not be disparaged as a motive.

But it is important to notice that there is a difference between, on the one hand, a person's actions functioning as a signal and, on the other, a person acting in order to signal. Signaling is an inevitable feature of observable behavior, whether it is intended or not. It is not inevitable, however, that we act to put on a display for others. Our concern is that people will behave worse when they aim to show off. If that's true, then a norm against such behavior could be an important safeguard for the efficacy of moral talk.

CONCLUSION

Moral talk is a tool. It has been used on some valuable, important, and impressive projects, but it is still only a tool. That moral talk has been, and continues to be, instrumental in making the world more just does not mean that every instance of moral talk must be associated with something morally valuable, or even morally permissible. Hammers can be used to drive and pull nails. They can also be used to assault people. No one over the age of three would cheer every swing of a hammer. Neither should they cheer every instance of moral talk.

Chapter 6

Would a Virtuous Person Grandstand?

To this point, our moral case against grandstanding has focused on the impact of grandstanding on other people. This should not be surprising. When most people think about morality, they think about how our behavior affects others. In chapter 4, we argued that grandstanding is wrong because it carries significant social costs, which we all bear when grandstanders abuse moral talk. In chapter 5, we argued that even setting aside its bad consequences, grandstanding is wrong for an additional reason: it treats others with a lack of respect.

But there is more to morality than assessments of our behavior and its effects on other people. We also make judgments about how morally good people themselves are. We say things like, "Jim is trustworthy," and "Kerry is selfish." In doing so, we assess others' moral character.

Thinking about character can illuminate important moral differences between people. Suppose Jamie donates her time at a homeless shelter. She plays cards with the homeless, helps them get medical care, and works to find them stable jobs. She enjoys this work and volunteers because she wants to help those who have hard lives. She has the character trait, or virtue, of compassion.

Will also volunteers at the shelter and does all the things Jamie does. However, he detests volunteering, and does it only because he is doing research for an acting role in a movie. He pretends quite convincingly that he cares, but he actually hates the homeless and wishes he could go back to ignoring them. Although Will and Jamie's behavior is, for all outward appearances, basically the same, there is a significant moral difference between them. Jamie is the more compassionate person. There are important moral qualities that are not necessarily revealed by our behavior.

Thinking about moral character not only helps us illuminate differences between people, it can also shed light on moral questions about how we should live. We might ask, for instance, whether a person with impeccable character would cheat on his taxes. How would a generous person treat her friends in need? In this chapter, we ask whether a virtuous person would grandstand.

Recall that our Basic Account of grandstanding includes the Recognition Desire: when someone grandstands, she is motivated to a significant degree by a desire that others think of her as morally respectable. Some readers might have noticed that none of the arguments we gave in previous chapters depended on there being anything wrong with having such a desire. Rather, the problems we have pointed out so far have been with the things people tend to *do* because they are motivated by the Recognition Desire. But we will go further than this. Having the Recognition Desire to the degree grandstanders do is a defect in a person's character.

Throughout the centuries, people have put forward many conceptions of virtue, and we will not pretend to cover them all here.[1] Instead, we will try out a few popular approaches and show that on all of them, grandstanding is typically not something a virtuous person would do. Let's start by examining a traditional conception of virtue, according to which a virtuous person does the right thing for the right reason.

DOING THE RIGHT THING FOR THE RIGHT REASON

Looking strictly at someone's outwardly observable behavior can tell us whether she does the right thing. But to know whether she is a good person, we must look deeper. Among other things, we must look at why she acts as she does.[2] What is her motivation?

Think again of Jamie and Will from our earlier example. Although Will did all the right things at the shelter, he was clearly not acting virtuously. He hates the homeless and volunteers only because he needs experience being around them to prepare for an acting gig. Being a virtuous person requires more than just doing the right things. According to the traditional view of the virtues, to be virtuous, you must do the right things for the right reasons.[3]

But what are the right reasons? What motivates a virtuous person? To answer this question, we can simplify matters and focus on three broad kinds of motivations for our actions.[4]

1. Egoistic Motivation: you are ultimately concerned with yourself and acting in your own interests.
2. Altruistic Motivation: you are ultimately concerned with what is good for other people.
3. Dutiful Motivation: you are ultimately concerned with doing your duty, or with what is morally right.

Let's return to the homeless shelter to illustrate these various motives. Jamie volunteers at the shelter because she wants the homeless to feel valued, listened to, and cared for. She wants to help them improve their diets and physical health. She works with them to find jobs because she wants them to improve their lot in life and take pride in contributing to society. In short, Jamie is moved to act as she does by a desire to help other people. Her motivations are altruistic. Of course, Jaime might also derive some additional personal benefits from volunteering—for instance, she can list this experience on her résumé. But if her motivation is altruistic, these benefits are by-products, rather than goals, of her action.

Alternatively, Jamie's motivations might have been dutiful. She might have been motivated by a concern to act in accordance with moral principles—to do the right thing simply because it is the right thing to do. We can imagine Jamie becoming convinced—by moral argument, her conscience, or religious teaching—that there is a moral imperative to help the poor. She might have volunteered simply because she knew she ought to do so.

Will's motivations, however, were egoistic. Ultimately, he doesn't care about the homeless. Will volunteers at the shelter because he thinks it will help him become a movie star. He actually hates the homeless and is just using them to further his career. If his fieldwork is helpful, he'll get rich, and finally be able to move to Miami and buy a fiberglass speed boat. Or consider Mary, who volunteers at the shelter because she hopes to be interviewed on local television and look like a moral hero. These motivations are neither altruistic nor dutiful.

Of course, real life is rarely this simple. As we explained in chapter 2, we usually act out of mixed motivations. We hope you will agree, however, that while it's easy to imagine a virtuous person volunteering at a homeless shelter for altruistic or dutiful reasons, it's difficult to imagine a virtuous person acting on motivations like Will's or Mary's. You might be deeply impressed by Will's or Mary's volunteer work. But surely you would downgrade your evaluation of their moral character if you learned that they volunteered so they could buy a speedboat or get on television. A well-behaved person might be useful to have around, but a person of excellent character is both useful and admirable.

Now that we have a grasp on what kinds of motivations are typical of a virtuous person on the traditional account, we can ask: would a virtuous person grandstand? A grandstander contributes to public discourse because of the Recognition Desire: she wants to be seen as morally respectable. But the Recognition Desire does not appear to be either an altruistic or a dutiful motivation. Instead, it appears egoistic: grandstanders want attention. They want to be seen as morally impressive.

Does this show that virtuous people wouldn't grandstand? We think the fact that grandstanders have significantly egoistic motivations when they engage in public discourse is good evidence that virtuous people would avoid grandstanding. But we also think that a stronger case can be made by appealing to the idea of civic virtue. Not all public moral discourse concerns politics or civil society, but the idea of a good citizen is a useful point of comparison for understanding what it means to contribute well to public discourse.

GRANDSTANDING AND CIVIC VIRTUE

Civic virtue is the "disposition to further public over private good in action and deliberation."[5] A good citizen is one who puts her own interests aside when called upon to do her civic duty to further the common good. Someone might fail to live up to this calling by using political institutions simply as a tool for advancing her own interests. For instance, someone who has invested heavily in military contractors might campaign for a candidate who supports going to war, simply because she wants her investments to thrive. Or perhaps worse, a politician might use political institutions to attack his critics. He might propose policies they dislike simply because they dislike them. Or he might try to set back their interests simply out of malice. Alternatively, someone might seek an important public office simply for his own self-aggrandizement, rather than out of any interest in the common good. These examples all concern people favoring their private interests over the public good. The motivations are egoistic, ultimately concerned with personal gain. In any of these ways, and many others, a person could pursue his private good exclusively, and thus fail to live up to the ideals of civic virtue.

There is a helpful comparison to be made between civic virtue and virtuous contribution to public moral discourse. Recall that we said a virtuous person will often have non-egoistic motivations. In politics, she might want to use state institutions to promote the well-being of others. In public moral discourse, she might want to help other people think more clearly and carefully about moral questions, or to advance arguments or take stands that encourage people to treat one another better.

Alternatively, a virtuous person might be motivated to act according to duty. In politics, she may want her state to enter a just war simply because it is the right thing to do, for instance. In public moral discourse, a person with this kind of motivation presents others with arguments simply because she wants people to have true moral beliefs. She wants others to act for the right reasons, like she strives to do herself.

Just as you would downgrade your assessment of someone's character if you found out her participation in politics was egoistically motivated, we think you should downgrade your judgment of someone's character if you found out she approaches public moral discourse egoistically. If someone uses public moral discourse to seek greater social status and make herself look impressive, for instance, she departs significantly from the motivations traditionally associated with virtue.

Think of a morally moving or inspiring speech—one that makes you think highly of the person who delivered it. Perhaps you will think of Gandhi's "Quit India" speech, or Martin Luther King's "I Have a Dream," or Sojourner Truth's "Ain't I a Woman." Whichever speech you find most inspiring, imagine the BBC reports today that archivists have turned up a long-lost diary by the figure who gave the speech, and it contains dozens of entries made as the figure prepared to deliver it. But there is little mention in those diary entries of the figure's hopes that the speech might turn the tide of public opinion toward the correct moral view, or that the speech might lead to a disadvantaged group getting the help it needs or the respect it deserves. Instead, what seems to have preoccupied the figure was an interest in securing his place in the historical record as a moral paragon, impressing potential romantic partners with his love of justice, and saying just the right combination of words to get quoted on activists' placards forever.

We probably have idealized views of what some of history's greatest heroes were like. People are complicated. In some respects, it wouldn't really matter much if the hero you had in mind used her moral talk egoistically. Unless she was egoistically motivated in most areas of her life, she would still probably be a good person—maybe even a great one. But the proof of her true motivations would shed disappointing light on her character. We would not say that such a person is fully virtuous

if she contributed to public moral discourse with those aims so promi-
nently in mind, even if her words had a tremendous positive impact on
the world. If what you care most about is showing that your heart is in
the right place, then your heart is not in the right place.[6]

But perhaps this reaction to the vain, fame-seeking hero is unduly harsh. We will now consider an alternative view of virtue, on
which the vain may be rated more favorably.

VIRTUES AND CONSEQUENCES

Some readers may have a more sympathetic reaction to the figure in
the diary scenario. Far from showing that the hypothetical hero was
flawed, they will say this case simply shows she was human. Human
beings are motivated by concerns for their legacy, their romantic
prospects, and their reputation among those they hold in esteem.
These are natural human desires, and it should not be surprising
that our heroes are wired much like the rest of us. But, these readers
might point out, there is an important lesson in the case: we can be
motivated to accomplish great things without having some rare set
of ideal character traits. Even egoistic concerns can motivate us to
do good in the world.

Some philosophers take this insight and use it to advance a very
different notion of the virtues than the one we have considered so
far. Rather than thinking of a virtuous person as one with character
traits that are excellent in themselves, they say we should think of
virtues as the character traits that lead to good consequences overall.
This view is called virtue consequentialism. It is an alternative to the
traditional view of virtue.[7] It gets its name because it says a trait is a
virtue when having it leads people to act in ways that produce more
good than bad consequences.[8]

For example, according to virtue consequentialism, honesty is a virtue because it causes people to do more good than bad in the world.[9] In other words, to determine whether something is a virtue, we shouldn't just consider some pattern of beliefs, desires, habits, and motivations and then ask whether that pattern is "virtuous" or not. Instead, we should look at the results of having that pattern of beliefs, desires, habits, and motivations. When a person is motivated by a particular trait, does she act in a way that typically produces overall good consequences? If so, then that trait is a virtue. The point is that you can't simply look at a trait and see whether it's a virtue. You must look at what that trait leads people to do. Suppose being honest systematically led people to act in ways that caused misery, pain, death, hurt feelings, and suffering. Would you still think it was a virtue—something that made someone a good person? Virtue consequentialists say no. To be virtuous is to have the traits that lead you to act in ways that have good consequences.

VANITY AS VIRTUE?

Let's now apply this way of thinking about character traits to grandstanding. Grandstanders want to gain recognition from others. As we saw in chapter 2, they are typically motivated by a sense of grandiosity and self-centeredness. Let's use the term "vanity" to refer to the trait that grandstanders tend to possess. Perhaps vanity is not quite what we would hope for from an ideal contributor to public moral discourse, as we argued earlier in this chapter. But we are now thinking of virtuous character traits differently. We are now asking whether the trait typically has more good than bad consequences. Could vanity be a virtue on this view? And if vanity is a virtue, wouldn't this mean that grandstanding is virtuous after all?

Eighteenth-century Scottish Enlightenment philosopher David Hume thought vanity—"the desire of reputation"—is useful in motivating us to do good in the world.[10] "Vanity," he wrote, is "to be esteemed a social passion, and a bond of union among men."[11] Why did Hume think this? He recognized that while virtually all of us care deeply for ourselves and our family and friends, few of us are motivated to help those more distant from us. We are greatly limited in our altruism. We like the idea of other people living well, but the idea of making great personal sacrifices to help distant others to live well appeals to us much less. So we need something else to motivate us to lift more than a finger to help other people—there must be something in it for us. Altruistic and dutiful motivations won't cut it.

Vanity is one way we can be moved more effectively to help others. Vain people care about what others think of them, and they deliberately take steps to curate a positive social image.[12] Because we evaluate one another partly on the basis of our moral qualities, some of that curation includes moral talk designed to show other people how good we are. Vanity can serve as a "bond of union" by driving us to create networks of esteem that can have important positive results. If vanity has such good consequences, this might be a good reason to think that it is a virtue after all. And if vanity is a virtue, one of its typical consequences—grandstanding—may turn out to be exactly the kind of thing a virtuous person would do.

IS GRANDSTANDING VIRTUOUS AFTER ALL?

Vanity drives people to grandstand, and in some ways that might be a good thing. Since it often involves the repeated recitation of claims about shared moral values, grandstanding can reaffirm and spread good social norms. Hearing other people say repeatedly that human lives are valuable—and chiming in to say so yourself—reminds you that there is widespread agreement about the value of human life. It also reminds you that others will look askance at behavior that fails to show the proper regard for human life, thus providing an added incentive to behave yourself. So grandstanding can both strengthen social norms and encourage people to act morally. Contrary to our earlier claim that grandstanding reveals a lack of virtue, have we now discovered that grandstanding is precisely what a virtuous person would do? If it's good to be vain, then isn't it good to grandstand? It is, after all, what the vain do.[13]

Imagine for the moment that vanity is a virtue because it generally produces good consequences overall. Even so, it doesn't follow that it is virtuous to act vainly in every situation you encounter. Some situations call for humility and modesty, even when your inclinations run in the other direction. It would be inappropriate to tell the hilarious story of the time you delivered a humiliating comeback to your mother-in-law while you are giving a eulogy at her funeral. The point is that even if vanity is generally a virtue, not all situations call for vain behavior.

By comparison, suppose that honesty is a virtue for precisely the reason the virtue consequentialist says it is: honesty motivates us to do things that have good consequences overall. Even if honesty is a virtue, it doesn't follow that a virtuous person would always do the honest thing. Sometimes, virtue requires doing something dishonest. Suppose the Gestapo asks if you are harboring Jews in your basement. Surely a virtuous person would not respond honestly in such a scenario.

A reasonable virtue consequentialist would not say that acting vainly is always virtuous. Rather, she will claim that the virtuous person will act vainly *in some situations*.[14] Since our concern here is grandstanding—vain action in the context of public discourse—we can simply focus our attention on the question of whether acting vainly has overall good consequences in public discourse.

Chapter 4 is devoted to answering that question. In those pages, we have already exposed some of the bad consequences of grandstanding. So we have come full circle. While there may be many contexts in which vanity has good consequences, acting on the Recognition Desire in public discourse causes considerable damage. It generally leads people not to treat each other well but instead to jockey for a better position among their peers and fight over whatever gains in status are there for the taking. It makes people seek out new opportunities to demonstrate their moral qualities, sacrificing the legitimate interests of others as they do so.

But a virtue consequentialist who still hopes to vindicate grandstanding could try one final argument. Suppose you thought some people know the truth about justice. It would be valuable for us all if they shared their knowledge in public discourse. But if there was nothing in it for them, they might not bother. On the other hand, if these people were vain, they could contribute their knowledge, support positive moral change, and get something for their trouble: recognition for being morally impressive. On this picture, vanity is a valuable trait to have in public discourse because it motivates people to share their beliefs about morality and contribute to important social movements.

But this rosy assessment of vanity relies on an incomplete consideration of its consequences. Vanity, in the form of the Recognition Desire, does not simply make it easier to say or do the right thing (if it does this at all). It motivates people to defend views or take action in order to garner positive attention, not because those views are true or because those actions are good. A desire to seek status can motivate people to grandstand instead of doing things that will have a greater moral impact.[15] It can even alter the kinds of moral projects to which we devote ourselves. Think back to the phenomenon of rage giving we discussed in chapter 4. Sure, getting people fired up in discussion because of their in-group's outrage might lead them to take action. But their energy will be directed toward what their group has identified as a worthwhile problem while grandstanding. Attention will be devoted to moral causes because they provide opportunities for grandstanding, not because they are important. While it is true that vanity can motivate some people to do the right thing in public discourse, we have argued that it is more likely to have bad consequences. Of course, you might think your vanity in public discourse generally leads to good consequences. But what makes you so special?

Even if virtue consequentialism is the correct approach to identifying virtues, there is no good reason to think that vanity produces better consequences in public discourse than other traits like modesty, humility, or civic virtue. So it seems that according to virtue consequentialism, a virtuous person will not grandstand.

GRANDSTANDING AND NIETZSCHE

Some readers might be in general agreement with our arguments in this chapter so far, yet also feel a sense of dissatisfaction. Sure, we've given some reasons to think that grandstanding doesn't meet the traditional virtue ethical standard of doing the right thing for the right reason. And the traits associated with grandstanding don't seem likely to win approval from virtue consequentialists. While these are satisfying enough accounts of why grandstanding shows a lack of virtue, some will think they just scratch the surface. Surely there's something sterner to be said about the character of grandstanders. After all, grandstanders frequently clothe their attempts to further their own interests in the language of concern for others, and use that same kind of talk as a socially acceptable way to abuse those they dislike. This is not run of the mill, imperfectly virtuous behavior. It is a distinct form of vice that is worth diagnosing and condemning in stronger terms.

For readers hoping for a harsher condemnation of grandstanding, we have just the thing. The nineteenth-century German philosopher Friedrich Nietzsche, in developing one of the most interesting critiques of conventional morality in the history of philosophy, argued that modern moral practices prevent human beings from reaching their full potential.[16] His reasons for thinking this apply in interesting ways to the phenomenon of grandstanding. We'll explain some of Nietzsche's ideas here to develop another take on the vices involved in grandstanding. While the analysis we offer is inspired by Nietzsche's work, we are not trying to figure out what Nietzsche himself would say about grandstanding. We also disagree with Nietzsche about whether conventional morality is a good thing. But we think his diagnosis of the nastiness of some moral practice is accurate in important ways, and we'll draw on those insights here to evaluate grandstanding.

Let's start with Nietzsche's idea of the will to power. Nietzsche claims that all animals, including human beings, are instinctively motivated to maximize their feelings of power—that is, the feeling you get when you overcome resistance to realizing your goals.[17] That resistance could come from an opponent, material circumstances, or any other practical difficulty. We despise this resistance because it is frustrating, but we also need it to feel the sense of accomplishment we get upon overcoming it.

Nietzsche also holds a view of the good life for human beings that present-day moral philosophers call perfectionism.[18] According to perfectionists, a good life is one of excellence in pursuing some objective set of goods—knowledge, deep relationships with others, the creation of works of great aesthetic value, and so on. There is no consensus about what items are on Nietzsche's list of worthwhile excellences, as his remarks on this point are characteristically cryptic, but he clearly emphasizes creativity, and frequently stresses the importance of a person "creating" herself. We need not settle this issue, though, because we are not interested primarily in Nietzsche's own view. The point is that if a person is living well, she will seek to overcome resistance as she pursues certain goals. Not just any goal will do, though. Some pursuits are unworthy of a person's time and energy. The fewer objective goods a person has in her life, the less well her life is going, even if she is satisfied with the things she pursues.

Nietzsche thinks we are not all equally good at pursuing excellence in life. Some people achieve great satisfaction in maximizing their feeling of power in attaining their goals, while others are frustrated—and sometimes greatly so. This is where the trouble starts. Rather than simply admit defeat, those who fail to exercise their will to power by achieving things that are actually worthwhile move the goalposts. They attempt to redefine what it is to live well and denigrate others' success. The result is what Nietzsche calls a "slave revolt" in morals. By that he means that the unsuccessful tell themselves that something about them is valuable as consolation for their failures. Consequently, Nietzsche thinks true human excellence is disvalued and denigrated. When a culture's sense of what is valuable shifts in response to these efforts, this leads to what Nietzsche called a "revaluation" of values. What had previously been seen as a mark of human failure becomes moral goodness. And what had previously been seen as human excellence becomes moral evil. What is crucial for our purposes is that the slave revolt involves people using morality itself to satisfy their will to power. Nietzsche thinks that our own culture has already undergone such a revolt. Thus, our dominant moral beliefs are badly mistaken, as they are designed to shame the strong and valorize the weak.[19]

On this overall, substantive evaluation of the state of common morality, we strongly disagree with Nietzsche. We think that some of the changes he decries—particularly the widespread recognition of all human beings as moral equals—are positive developments, and even great cultural achievements. In fact, there is much we have said in this book that Nietzsche would have rejected. But even though we disagree with Nietzsche about some things, we think he offers an important insight about morality in general: people frequently use morality to feel powerful, and even to exert their will over others. Indeed, this insight can help us think about grandstanding in a new light.

As we have been at pains to show throughout this book, people often use morality—and especially moral talk—for egoistic, self-serving ends. We said at the start of the book that moral talk is not magic, but it can be a kind of trick. People use moral talk in underhanded ways to promote their own interests, just as Nietzsche would predict. We also think he is right about why people use morality this way—to raise their status, to gain some sense of satisfaction that they are achieving something in the world. The lesson we draw is not that commonsense morality is deeply mistaken, but that moral talk is often a sheepskin worn by weak or desperate wolves. They cannot get what they want through a direct act of strength— by actually achieving excellence to the degree they desire—so they find another way. They instead tell themselves that being seen as a good person is a worthwhile achievement, and then put their self-enhanced moral qualities on display. It is a cunning gambit, in a way, but it is also underhanded, and often cruel. It might make them feel powerful, but their achievement is empty.[20] Impressing others through grandstanding is not the same as actually achieving excellence.

But why isn't getting recognition from others for having good moral qualities a goal worth pursuing? We mentioned earlier that our own empirical studies suggest that grandstanders pursue two kinds of status: prestige, or the status that comes from people thinking well of you for your knowledge, skills, or success; and dominance, the status you get by instilling fear in others through intimidation, coercion, or displays of brute force.

Let's first consider grandstanding to dominate others. Dominance grandstanding involves raising oneself up by tearing other people down. These grandstanders try to seize social power by treating morality as a weapon. That this comes so close to being exactly what Nietzsche describes as a slave revolt in morals should make clear why it cannot be part of a worthy goal. Just as the original "slave revolt" sought to use morality as a tool to dominate others, grandstanders use morality—and especially moral talk—to seize the high ground. Dominance grandstanding is a way of sacrificing others in an attempt to exercise one's will to power.

Now take grandstanding to gain prestige. This type of grandstanding often involves reassuring the in-group that you are like them, and therefore of value. A Nietzschean will wonder of these grandstanders: isn't there some other way of demonstrating your value? The rote recitation of moral terms that people approve of seems like a cheap substitute for a more worthwhile display of what makes you an interesting person worth listening to or associating with. The same is true for more ambitious forms of prestige grandstanding. If you want to demonstrate not just that you belong, but that you are fit for a prominent role in a group, falling back on the crutch of moral talk as a way of demonstrating your value is a strategy for the weak. Real excellence is harder, but it is more rewarding, and also more honest.

From a Nietzschean perspective, grandstanding is not something an excellent person would do. Excellent people devote their time and energy to worthwhile goals—goals that are good for human beings to attain. We need not agree with Nietzsche about what those goals are. We might, for example, think that pleasure, knowledge, achievement, moral virtue, and relationships are central worthwhile human goals.[21] Whatever they happen to be, we think that Nietzsche was right about at least this much: an excellent person will not use morality, including moral talk, as a tool to satisfy her will to power. An excellent person, therefore, would not grandstand. Excellent people have no interest in petty attempts to gain status through strategic uses of moral talk.

CONCLUSION

We have now come to the end of our arguments against grandstanding. In previous chapters, we focused on grandstanding's bad consequences and the ways it fails to treat others with sufficient respect. In this chapter, we approached the ethics of grandstanding from a different angle, by asking how a virtuous person would behave in public discourse. We showed that on the traditional view of virtue, you would think less of someone's character if you found she was egoistically using moral talk to promote her private interests over the public good. This is evidence that grandstanding is not something a virtuous person would do. We also considered an alternative approach, which says a trait is a virtue because it produces good consequences. We noted that even if vanity were a virtue in general, acting vainly in public discourse tends to have all the bad consequences we described in chapter 4. It would therefore not be virtuous to approach public discourse as a vehicle for self-promotion. Finally, we issued our harshest condemnation by appealing to Nietzsche's insights about the manipulative use of morality to argue that grandstanding is a pathetic and underhanded way of trying to feel powerful.

Chapter 7

Politics as Morality Pageant

Perhaps more than any other group, politicians are notorious for grandstanding. We see headlines accusing politicians of grandstanding all the time:

> "Politicians Must Stop the Grandstanding and Start Addressing the Realities"[1]
>
> "The 'Protect and Serve Act' Is Political Grandstanding over a Nonexistent Problem—And It Could Cause Real Harm"[2]
>
> "Obama Attacks Republican 'Grandstanding'"[3]
>
> "President Obama's Grandstanding on Signing Statements"[4]

This should come as no surprise. Politicians are, after all, in the public eye because they wield, or at least hope to wield, political power. With that territory comes the frequent expression of beliefs about what is wrong with the world, and how things ought to be. In other words, offering up soundbites of moral talk for public consumption is part of a politician's job description. In democracies, politicians have an interest in cultivating a favorable public image. They want to get elected. They also want to gain public support for their preferred policies and legislation. So their moral talk is usually designed to elicit public support. Of course, politicians are not the only political actors. Political activists, for instance, also want to sway public opinion, mobilize political support, and influence politicians and other activists.

We will use the term *political grandstanding* to refer to the moral grandstanding that politicians and other political actors (such as activists) engage in as part of their political activities. In this chapter, we explore the question of what happens to politics in a democracy when political grandstanding is rewarded.

An exhaustive answer to this question would take a whole book itself. So we will just focus on three negative consequences of grandstanding for politics in democracies. But before we get into those issues, let's discuss why politicians are such prominent grandstanders to begin with.

WHY DO POLITICIANS GRANDSTAND?

It is easy to denounce politicians' grandstanding. It often appears so nakedly self-serving and craven. But if we take a step back and consider the incentives politicians face, their grandstanding seems more understandable, and maybe even inescapable. Politicians grandstand more than most people, we suggest, because they have more incentives to do so. Like many others, politicians have narcissistic tendencies. But electoral politics offers a ready, eager, and demanding audience the likes of which most of us will never have to face. As political scientists Peter Hatemi and Zoltán Fazekas note:

> Politics arguably presents the ideal theater for narcissism to be expressed: The endless trading of insults by politicians; the anxiety-laden, personalized, and alarmist mobilization messages propagated by campaigns; the demands that one group's needs

are more important or legitimate than others'; and the intrinsic rewards people obtain from watching the champions of their cause degrade their opponents put narcissism on display and [activate] it in the public like few other vehicles can.[5]

Political grandstanding has higher stakes than the grandstanding you see from your friends. Grandstanding political actors are not merely trying to win arguments, silence their opponents, or preen on social media. If a politician's grandstanding is successful, she can sway enough donors to run a strong campaign. She can earn the trust of enough voters to get elected. These and other factors give her enough clout to persuade or pressure colleagues to vote a certain way on legislation. And when political activists' grandstanding is successful, they can mobilize thousands—or even millions—of people to protest. On the other hand, if a politician fails to impress enough of the right people, he loses financial support from his party, political capital, and votes at the ballot box. Ultimately, he gets fired. Activists, especially professional activists, face similar worries.[6] Most of us are unlikely to have to grapple with these problems, not only because we lack the social visibility to influence so many people, but also because there is virtually zero chance that we will ever wield political power.

Politicians know that a lot rides on impressing voters. They also know how much voters want a morality pageant.[7] In one AP poll, most respondents said that "character" issues were more important than "policy" issues.[8] A CNN/USA Today/Gallup survey found that the most important trait in predicting how someone will vote for President is the extent to which a candidate shares the voter's values.[9] According to one Democratic Party strategist, "Modern day presidential campaigns are essentially character tests, with character broadly defined to encompass a mosaic of traits—looks, likability, vision, philosophy, ideology, biography, communications skills, intel-ligence, strength, optimism, empathy, ethics, values, among others."[10] Political scientists, too, have noted that campaigns are largely about convincing voters that candidates possess certain character traits.[11]

Why do many voters care about supporting politicians they think are morally good? After all, a morally suspect but smart, ca-pable, well-educated person could be just as efficient at enacting the "right" policies. One reason is that voters may just prefer to be represented by morally good people. Politicians "speak for" their constituents, and constituents might want their representative to have high character. Or maybe people want to avoid supporting a morally bad person in her endeavors, no matter how efficient she might be at reforming the tax code.

Others may use a politician's character as a proxy for something else. It takes a lot of time and energy to figure out not only what the best policies are, but which politician is best-suited to enact them. Some voters might reason that since the better person will enact better policies, it's easier just to assess candidates' character and vote for the better person.[12] So they simply vote for whoever seems to have certain desirable moral traits.[13]

Whatever their reasons, many people base their votes on the moral character or shared values of politicians. We won't take a stand about whether people should vote on the basis of candidates' character or values.[14] But just as a matter of fact, most people are not informed enough to choose candidates on the basis of their level of knowledge or policy expertise.[15] Our point is simply that many people do cast their votes based on their judgments about candidates' character. Like former President Richard Nixon, they think: "You must not give power to a man unless, above everything else, he has character. Character is the most important qualification the President of the United States can have."[16]

Because the public cares about character, politicians recognize a demand for displays of their moral qualities. If you want to know that your senator cares deeply for the poor, then she'll show you just how much she cares. This demand for moral displays turns politics into a morality pageant.

Because voters demand that politicians display their moral credentials, we do not deny that moral grandstanding can be very effective at achieving political ends, even good ones. This might mean that grandstanding is morally permissible for politicians more often than it is for the rest of us. We will return to this issue at the end of the chapter. But however effective political grandstanding might be, such grandstanding still has costs of its own. After all, lying can also be an effective way to accomplish political goals. The same could be true of imprisoning the opposition. But it would be unreasonable to defend the morality of these practices by saying, "Hey, it gets the people I like elected!"

Grandstanding in politics is an effective tool for some purposes. It might even be impossible to eliminate. We should recognize that the reason grandstanding works is that people *want* their politicians to put on a morality pageant. But the fact that some people watch the pageant is not a compelling argument in its defense. It imposes significant costs on us all, and if people saw those costs more clearly, perhaps they would stop incentivizing political grandstanding. In the rest of the chapter, we identify three costs of political grandstanding in a democracy.

THE NO COMPROMISE PROBLEM

A classic criticism of democracies is that they devolve into a war between factions—polarized groups that aim to promote their own interests at the expense of others.[17] One vital tool for preventing this fate—or at least delaying it—is a healthy public discourse. Healthy discourse allows individuals and groups to confront their shared problems and grievances with one another openly, and deliberate about how to handle them. Such discourse depends on certain background cultural conditions: low costs of self-expression, norms of sincerity, space for reasonable disagreement, some degree of open-mindedness, and social trust, to name a few.[18] We have already shown how grandstanding interferes with some of these values. For instance, it undermines trust between citizens by encouraging cynicism and apathy about public moral discourse. And common manifestations of grandstanding like ramping up and trumping up promote group polarization.

Grandstanding in politics contributes to what we call the No Compromise Problem: grandstanding undermines conditions that could lead to compromise between opposing political groups. Grandstanding thus makes democracies more vulnerable to the dangers of factions. Grandstanding does not just contribute to group polarization. It also makes it harder for members of opposing groups to put aside their differences and make deals to solve problems on terms that enough people can accept. So grandstanding does more than create divisions in a society. It also makes those divisions difficult to overcome by crowding out broad bases of appeal. We can see how grandstanding undermines the possibility of compromise by looking at two common ways grandstanding is used in politics: (1) in-group appeals and (2) out-group attacks.

When political actors grandstand by making in-group appeals, they try to show the politically like-minded that they share their values. This often takes the form of showing others that they are ideologically pure, or more ideologically pure than, say, rival politicians within their own party. Displays of ideological purity are often moral in character. One can easily imagine, for instance, a politician saying that anyone who really cared about justice would support a $15 per hour minimum wage. These kinds of moral claims serve a political purpose. They place the person who makes them in the vanguard of her in-group—the select few who push the group into adopting new, radical views. Those who stake out new moral ground like this can be trusted not to backtrack. For many partisans, this is music to their ears. Ideological purity holds more value to them than does willingness to compromise to get things done. It is not encouraging for the party faithful to hear from a potential leader that she is willing to compromise on the values that make her an attractive candidate to them in the first place.

Sometimes you will even see a politician brag about his refusal to compromise as a show of ideological purity. Unsurprisingly, these statements are usually made as in-group appeals. When he first ran for U.S. Senate, Ted Cruz told a crowd of Texans during the Republican primary, "If you're looking for an established moderate who will go to Washington and work across the aisle and compromise . . . I'm not the guy."[19] Cruz was referring to his opponent, Republican David Dewhurst's apparent openness to supporting the Democratic Party-sponsored Affordable Care Act: "Nobody looking at David Dewhurst's record in the Texas legislature can doubt for a moment that he would run, not walk, to the middle to those advocating compromise in the Senate." Cruz won that Senate seat.

Cruz sees his job as defending what is plainly right, rather than working with the other side: "I don't think what Washington needs is more compromise, I think what Washington needs is more common sense and more principle."[20] This sort of talk is, no doubt, music to the ears of those who agree with Cruz about the contents of common sense. One occasionally even hears political opponents say that they admire the sentiment being expressed—of favoring principle over pragmatism. It is, they say, a welcome change from all those on the wrong side of history who take stances solely out of greed, perversion, or other base motives.

The problem we want to emphasize is that the more a political issue becomes moralized, the less likely people are to compromise on that issue. Political scientist Timothy Ryan found that people are much less likely to compromise on an issue once they turn it into a matter of moral conviction, those deeply held moral attitudes that we discussed in chapter 3.[21] The more your views on Social Security reform, collective bargaining rights, stem-cell research, or same-sex marriage are part of your core, fundamental moral convictions, the less open to compromise you will be about them.

This is why grandstanding undermines the possibility of political compromise. As we have seen, grandstanding often involves moralizing: the illicit application of morality where it doesn't belong, or the exaggeration of moral claims. Moralizing transforms run-of-the-mill issues into moral ones. Moralizers constantly seek out new areas of life to apply their superior moral insight, and there is competitive pressure to make these concerns ever more fundamental to one's moral convictions. The field of issues about which people have moral convictions therefore expands. The more moral convictions expand and strengthen due to grandstanding, the more difficult it is for people to compromise.

This is dangerous. Political actors need only encourage the development of moral convictions about issues that are not even relevant or important for the lives of their in-group, and group members will respond by adopting an unyielding stance. As Robert Dahl warns, "To the man of rigid morality ... it is better not to agree at all than to agree to an imperfect bargain."[22]

There is a good reason for circumspect politicians to avoid making lots of absolute statements or taking moral stances willy-nilly. Why? Because when politicians take a moral stance, people expect them to stick to it. And when they appear to change their minds or back out on their commitments, voters punish them, viewing them as less worthy of support and less effective in their role.[23] Audiences expect the strength of moral commitments not to waver when new information becomes known, as pragmatic commitments might.[24] But as any competent moral philosopher will know, this is ridiculous. What we morally ought to do in any given case depends on facts about the world, just like considerations of prudence or efficiency can change given the discovery of new facts. Should we go to war? Institute a carbon tax? Abolish the minimum wage? The answer to all these questions depends in part on the facts on the ground. The amount of collateral damage and the number of likely civilian deaths matter as we try to settle the moral question of what to do. Furthermore, our best evidence of what the facts are often changes. That doesn't mean there is no moral truth about these questions. It just means the answer is hard to determine, and reasonable people—including politicians—should change their minds as the evidence changes.

But because people expect moral claims to be set in stone, grandstanding can interfere with a political actor's ability to govern. By giving an audience what it wants by grandstanding, or by trying to outflank in-group competition by displaying one's ideological purity, grandstanders risk boxing themselves in when they should instead preserve their flexibility. In other words, politicians might need to change course to do the right thing, and yet be prevented from doing so because they took a hardline moral stance to display their ideological purity. Grandstanding aimed at one's fellow partisans may then not only prevent politicians from being able to compromise with the other side, it may also prevent them from doing the right thing by their constituents—or not without significant backlash, at any rate.

Political grandstanding may also take the form of an attack on out-groups. The strategy is to draw sharp contrasts between the grandstander and the out-group, such as those in an opposing political party. The other side hates minorities, but you love and welcome everyone. You care about hard work and responsibility; they reward sloth. You are a selfless civil servant; they are in the pockets of big banks. You want a verdant and peaceful world; they want a violent, fascist ethnostate. You want to preserve your culture's language and customs; they want to institute Sharia Law.

Grandstanding through out-group attacks often takes the form of presenting a caricature of your opponents. A single bogeyman serves as a symbolic stand-in for the whole group. The bogeyman is often a person with publicly known vices that may be entirely incidental to her moral or political views. He might even be relatively unimportant to the cause or political movement he is supposed to represent. Think, for instance, of the way some conservatives in the United States still refer to former President John F. Kennedy's extramarital affairs as evidence of rot at the heart of the contemporary Democratic Party, or pick on and repeat ill-informed activist remarks from Hollywood liberals as if they represent the best the other side can offer.

Progressives have their pick of fringe conservative media figures—Ann Coulter, Tomi Lahren, Alex Jones—to inflate in importance until they are seen as emblematic of a dysfunctional right wing. Grandstanders frequently invoke names like these to boost their own status. The usual idea is that "this is the kind of person we're up against."

Bogeymen grandstanding accomplishes two things. First, it communicates that the out-group is too vicious to be trusted, since they welcome the bogeyman as one of their own. Second, it intimates that the grandstander and her audience are not only morally better than such people, but also united in opposition to them. Perhaps the grandstander will even protect his audience from the hated figure and the movement she represents. Neither of these messages bodes well for potential compromise with those on the other side who are not bogeymen.

Similarly, grandstanders have an incentive to draw attention to the most objectionable fringe policy proposals of the out-group and pretend that they represent the core of that group's agenda. Politicians can use this "fringe-idea grandstanding" to maximize the popular sense of the threat posed by the out-group. Fringe-idea grandstanding also makes the grandstander seem like the champion of the group under siege. For example, conservatives in the United States frequently express concerns that the left has plans (sometimes secret ones, at that) to use state institutions to seize all personally owned firearms, which many rank-and-file conservatives regard as a doomsday scenario.[25] Warnings of imminent seizures reach a fever pitch after mass shootings.

Progressives, meanwhile, fixate on the most outrageous policy suggestions floated by any conservative in response to a mass shooting, and treat them as a plausible legislative outcome and existential threat, too. As we write this, progressives are keeping on life support their outrage about some on the right—including President Trump—toying with the idea of requiring teachers to carry guns to defend against school shootings. The task of painting the other side's policy agenda as extremist is made easier, of course, when the out-group engages in ramping up to the point that they actually are advocating absurd fringe policies. By pointing out the danger posed by the enemy, the grandstander can build a reputation as someone who is sensitive to threats that others might overlook or fail to take seriously. Naturally, the grandstander's concerns might be just as effective even if they are trumped up, or otherwise uncharitable representations of what the other side is up to. Fringe-idea grandstanding makes compromise more difficult, too. When the most extreme partisan ideas are used to represent a whole out-group, any compromise with that group looks like a deal with the devil.

Finally, a grandstander might promote her status within her in-group by portraying even the mainstream values of the out-group as extreme and alien to her own group. Call this alienation grandstanding. If a case can be made that even the mainstream members of the out-group hold extreme values, then the grandstander's in-group will see it as a greater threat. They will also, again, see the in-group and its defenders as increasingly important. By drawing attention to the out-group's extremism and expressing disapproval of it, grandstanders display their value to the in-group.

This dynamic is unfortunately common between the contemporary right and left in American politics. Conservative commentator Kurt Schlichter unwittingly offers the following paradigmatic example of alienation grandstanding:

> They hate you. Leftists don't merely disagree with you. They don't merely feel you are misguided. They don't think you are merely wrong. They hate you. They want you enslaved and obedient, if not dead. Once you get that, everything that is happening now will make sense. And you will understand what you need to be ready to do.
>
> You are normal, and therefore a heretic. You refuse to bow to their idols, to subscribe to their twisted catechisms, to praise their false gods. This is unforgivable. You must burn.[26]

More specifically, many on the right claim that the left has planned all along not only to have the state recognize gay marriages as being on equal footing with traditional heterosexual marriages, but to undermine traditional sexual morality entirely. They insist that the left's claim to want the state "out of the bedroom" rests on a principle far more radical than a mere demand for equal recognition of partnerships between consenting adults. If the liberalization of sexual morality goes unchecked, they say, the left will eventually call for the toleration of bestiality and pedophilia.

Meanwhile, the left has recently discovered Margaret Atwood's 1985 dystopian novel *The Handmaid's Tale*, in which the United States government has been overthrown by a theocratic Christian regime that institutes misogynistic laws and practices, including sexual slavery. Some activists on the left now appear at protests wearing the red habits and white bonnets of the handmaids in the novel, representing their fear that the real agenda of the right is to strip them of their human rights.[27] Some on the left even insist that in some ways, we are already living in *The Handmaid's Tale*.[28]

To be fair, one can usually find people in the out-group who are eager to embrace the extreme policies or values that grandstanders exploit when they make out-group attacks. One of the most incredible gifts of the internet is that fears presented as slippery slope arguments are often immediately confirmed by a zealot who is happy to follow even a caricature of her group's argument anywhere it might lead. But all this really shows is that some people are too quick to dig in and defend their team no matter the cost.

Out-group attacks like the ones we have described are counterproductive for consensus building. When the in-group becomes convinced that the out-group is full of people who are fundamentally opposed to them on moral and political matters, they come to think of themselves at least partly in negative terms—that is, as being not like the out-group.[29] When this tendency is coupled with the in-group purity tests, the prospects for compromise look grim. Even if a political actor sees grounds for shallow agreement between his group and the out-group, reaching across the aisle leaves him open to grandstanding attacks from the purest ideologues in his in-group. Those on the other side who are open to cooperation with him face the same vulnerability.

We do not mean to suggest, of course, that it is always appropriate to seek compromise with the "other side." On some issues, it would be wrong to compromise. Philosopher Avishai Margalit proposes the idea of a "rotten" compromise to describe such cases. A rotten compromise is a "compromise we should not make, come what may."[30] An example of a rotten compromise would be an agreement to establish or maintain an inhuman regime. Although we must sometimes make concessions to reach an agreement with political opponents we still need to live with, we should not strike compromises that involve things like making slavery legally permissible.[31] Margalit's distinction between types of compromise is helpful, as most reasonable people can recognize that not all of their group's favored policies concern the protection of basic human rights, and so can be tabled for the sake of securing peaceful cooperation. But for those who are most polarized, in part because of grandstanding, the opposing party will all too often represent an inhuman regime. For such people, *all* compromises are rotten compromises. When everything is a matter of fundamental moral principles, there can be no justification for "picking your battles" and taking what you can get. Yet sometimes we must try to strike even unfair compromises if doing so would prevent an even worse outcome.[32] But for the grandstander, any such compromise is complicity with evil and therefore unconscionable.

Fortunately, there are countervailing forces built into democratic institutions that make compromise politically savvy. Parties have an incentive to nominate "electable" candidates—ones that can appeal to voters outside the diehard partisans. Otherwise, they won't win elections, and will thus fail to hold institutional power. By the same logic, candidates have an incentive to appeal to the median voter, to secure as much of the vote as possible and maximize their chances at winning elections.[33] But campaign officials also sometimes speak of "base" elections, in which the winning strategy is to maximize turnout of your own supporters, and depress turnout from the opposition, rather than appeal to the other side.[34] So institutional incentives can help, but they are no replacement for a reasonable mass public.

When we demand that our politicians grandstand, we make it more difficult for them to compromise. We demand rigid ideological purity and reward politicians for showing that they are morally pure. We brand as traitors to the cause those who waver from our party's values. We cheer credulously when politicians come across well in statements they didn't write and in contrived publicity stunts. And we love it when they stand up to and question the moral integrity of out-groups. Is it any surprise, then, that so few politicians reach across the aisle to work out compromises with the other side?

THE EXPRESSIVE POLICY PROBLEM

When politics becomes a matter of symbolic gestures to show that your heart is in the right place, a politician will support policies simply because they express certain moral values. She might, for example, support open borders to show she is welcoming and compassionate. Another politician argues for war to show he values his country's honor. You can even imagine a politician supporting a policy simply because she thinks it shows she's on the right side of history, whatever that means. For similar reasons, politicians will object to policies that do not express certain values. Or perhaps they will object simply because a policy expresses the values of the "other side."[35]

When politics becomes a morality pageant, politicians support policies for the wrong reasons. We call this The Expressive Policy Problem, and it is the second of the three major problems grandstanding poses for politics.

Before we can understand the problem, we must explain what it means for behavior to express a value. Expressive behavior is behavior intended to express commitment to a moral principle without that behavior actually following that moral principle.[36] An example will make this idea clearer. Consider the wedding ring. In many cultures, wearing a wedding ring expresses the value of loyalty to a spouse. The ring signifies that you care about or are committed to the value of marital fidelity. But you aren't loyal to your spouse simply *because* you wear a ring. Wearing a wedding ring expresses a commitment to fidelity, but wearing the ring isn't itself an act of fidelity. Refusing to cheat is an act of fidelity. Of course, it might turn out that people who wear wedding rings *are* more faithful to their spouses, but their actual fidelity is a further fact about them. Wearing the ring merely expresses a value.

All of this might be true of policies, as well. Supporting a policy can express a value when your support is intended to communicate that you care about or are committed to that value.[37] For example, suppose there is a political party whose core value is that housing should be affordable for all. The party might express its commitment to that value by promoting rent control laws—a legally imposed upper limit on the amount landlords can charge for rent. Whether the rent control policy succeeds in making housing affordable for all is a separate issue from what the policy expresses.[38] Just like wearing a wedding ring doesn't necessarily mean you are faithful to your spouse, publicly supporting and passing rent control laws doesn't necessarily mean you are making housing affordable for all.

It might seem strange to think that some people form policy preferences on the basis of what those policies express, rather than what they actually do. So why do people give weight to expressiveness?

A popular explanation that we can adapt from the social sciences starts from the fact that information is costly to acquire, and information about politics and public policy is no exception.[39] Suppose you are a responsible person who wants to do your part as a citizen and make informed contributions to your civic culture. That goal involves a lot of work. To be informed about the state of the world, you must follow the news. If you are to be confident you're getting a clear picture of the day's events, you must get your news from multiple diverse sources, thinking critically about the difference in presentation as you read or watch.

And it isn't enough just to follow current events. You must also study at least recent history to understand the significance of what is happening now. And then there is still the question of what should be done. Even supposing the right answer to that question in any particular case is simple, knowing how to address your political community's problems requires considerable knowledge of potential policy devices, each of which comes with complicated costs and benefits. Researchers could fill the Library of Congress with things that almost no one knows—and actually, they have.[40]

It is unrealistic to think that even a conscientious person could acquire all the information just listed. And even if it were possible, it would almost certainly be irrational for anyone to do so. Life is full of things to do. Our lives (i.e., the authors') have been relatively uneventful and, frankly, lacking in excitement. We have weird interests, and we should probably both get out more. But even we have ways of seeking value in life that have far greater returns than reading about politics and public policy. Even if we were intensely interested in those subjects (we aren't), the practical effect of our knowing about them is inconsequential. In all but a few extreme outlier cases, even the highly politically knowledgeable produce little good for all the time they spend studying all these things. Further, the chance that any one person's vote will be decisive in an election of any significance, or contribute in any meaningful way to the margin of victory, is vanishingly small. In short, building the knowledge base of a good citizen is prohibitively costly. Your time would be better spent being a better parent, friend, sibling, co-worker, or just doing something for your own sake. That is in fact how most people allocate their time, and rationally so.

But many people who haven't done their reading are active in politics. To get around their lack of expertise, they make use of various heuristics, or rules of thumb, to aid them in their decision-making. An example of such a heuristic, and perhaps the most commonly used one, is party affiliation of candidates. Not sure who to vote for or why? Vote for candidates from the party that more frequently expresses your values.

Perhaps an even more fundamental heuristic is whether a candidate (or party) seems to care about you. It might be impossible for the average voter to tell what the long-run consequences of some technical policy might be, but people have a much stronger intuitive sense of whether a person is looking out for them—or, maybe more accurately, people feel like they have such a sense.

Members of the public who lack policy expertise will prefer policies that address the problems they care about in ways that are easy to understand. Why? As philosophers Guido Pincione and Fernando Tesón argue, "people are more likely to believe *vivid* theories of society," because "they trade on readily available 'evidence' that fits into our unreflective theoretical mindset."[41] They use the term "vivid" as psychologists do, to refer to information that is "(a) emotionally interesting, (b) concrete and imagery-provoking, and (c) proximate in a sensory, temporal, or spatial way."[42] For instance, suppose people are considering two possible explanations for the fact that a legislature, full of well-dressed and apparently well-to-do politicians, failed to pass some critical piece of legislation. On the one hand, these politicians might have failed because they are all "crooked." On the other, they might have acted under a complex set of conflicting—but perfectly above-board—incentives that made it irrational to pass any of the available options into law. The "crooked" explanation is vivid—it sparks indignation and calls to mind images of bags of money changing hands, which also explains why they can afford to dress so well. The complex incentives explanation is opaque. It is harder to describe, and it would require more details than anyone is in the mood to hear to be fully understood. Thus, vivid explanations tend to be more appealing.[43]

Political actors have an incentive to promote expressive policies that appeal to vivid explanations. Such policies express the values of their in-group more clearly, and thus are more effective as tools for self-promotion. Supporting expressive policies shows your in-group that you care about people like them, and that your heart is in the right place. Thus, expressive policies are attractive for grandstanders. And less expressive policies are unattractive by the same reasoning.

Unfortunately, while policies based on vivid explanations are appealing at first glance, they are frequently ineffective. Sometimes they are even counterproductive. This should not be surprising. The world is complicated. Consider again the problem of affordable housing shortages. Rent control policies address that problem vividly. The rent is too high, so why not just force landlords to charge less—or at least limit their capacity to raise rent further still? But as any student of basic economics can tell you, rent control policies lead to housing shortages. To take advantage of locked-in rental rates, people stop moving, and developers stop building new housing because they can earn greater returns on investment elsewhere.[44] The policies don't work. But grandstanding about them does. Politicians could hit the books until they figure out how to solve a problem and then try to explain it to an impatient in-group. Or they could come up with slogans and either promise or demand results right now in a ham-fisted way that sounds good but doesn't work.[45]

Examples abound. In 2012, Republicans in the Iowa state legislature attempted to decline nearly $2 billion in federal funding for Medicaid because that program had funded twenty-two abortions in the state. All the abortions were performed for reasons accepted by many pro-life activists as grounds for permissible abortion.[46] This move would allow candidates to say they pulled out all stops to defend the unborn—a vivid expression of their commitment to life—though the sudden loss of that much funding almost certainly would have been disastrous for other vulnerable people in their state.

Needle exchange programs allow people—typically drug users—to trade used hypodermic needles for clean ones. These programs are effective at preventing the spread of HIV and hepatitis, among other things. They are also another frequent target of grandstanders looking for opportunities to propose expressive policies. The usual move against such programs is to argue that they condone or even encourage immoral behavior. Advocates for these programs have mountains of empirical evidence showing that needle exchanges are effective at preventing the spread of disease and do not increase drug use.[47] But grandstanders need material, and a lot of people don't care much about drug addicts. So when the opportunity arises to criticize needle exchange programs, grandstanders suddenly seem concerned to keep their hands clean.

Perhaps you will disagree with us about some, or even all, of these examples. Maybe the politicians in question are raising valid moral concerns, and they are advocating for good political solutions. But nothing about our argument hinges on being right about these specific cases. The problem arises simply when politicians and voters focus on what a policy expresses instead of what it does. Remember: just because a policy expresses a value, that doesn't mean the policy actually promotes that value. Even worse, expressive policies often undermine the values they express.

This is not to say that there can be no good in expressing values, or in voters learning what values a politician has (assuming the politician is honestly expressing her values by supporting certain policies). We will return to this shortly. The harm, however, occurs when voters assume that if a politician supports a policy expressing some desirable value, enacting that policy would succeed in promoting that value. Voters should not conclude that a politician will advance their values just because they support policies that express those values. Voters should want a politician who advances policies that would actually advance their values.

But how can you tell whether a politician supports a policy simply because its expressive value makes her look good? Here's a test that will identify many cases: is the politician willing to disclose the expected bad consequences of her policy proposal? Pincione and Tesón call this the Display Test.[48] Virtually any policy proposal would have downsides—perhaps even significant ones—if implemented. If a politician is honest about these downsides and supports the policy anyway, this is good evidence that she supports the policy because she thinks it will secure overall good outcomes. On the other hand, if a politician obscures or refuses to acknowledge the negatives of her proposal, Pincione and Tesón suggest she is either ignorant or dishonest. She's ignorant if she's not aware of the downsides. She's dishonest if she's aware of the downsides but conceals them for a rhetorical advantage. As Pincione and Tesón put it, she's a "posturer."[49]

When we demand that our politicians grandstand, it is hardly surprising when they support policies that express the values we care about, regardless of whether those policies would accomplish their intended goals. This is why the Expressive Policy Problem is a problem. Because we care about expressive value, we end up supporting the wrong policies. The incentive for politicians is not to do the right thing, but to do what will gain them favor with the right people. If we offer them gains in status for making expressive policy proposals, they will give us what we're asking for: policies that sound good and don't work.

THE PARADOX OF SOLVING
SOCIAL PROBLEMS

Let's note one final danger of rewarding grandstanding in politics. The point of political action is to solve problems, not to create a forum for the glorification of those who participate. But if politics becomes a morality pageant, then the contestants have an incentive to keep problems intact—or perhaps even worse, to engage in political activism with no clear aim at all. We predict that the more politics becomes a forum to show off your moral qualities, the more people will be dedicated to activism for its own sake, simply as a vehicle to preen.

Consider the following passage from political theorist Michaele Ferguson about the Occupy movement:

> The activists involved have wagered on political freedom itself rather than a clear, common agenda as the focal point of the movement. One observer described the aim of Occupy actions in Zuccotti Park as establishing "a long-term encampment in a public space, an improvised democratic protest village without preappointed leaders, committed to a general critique—the U.S. economy is broken, politics is corrupted by big money— but with no immediate call for specific legislative or executive action." Given how quickly the 2006 immigration protests dissolved once the organizers' common goals were achieved, this may be a smart political strategy. *If Occupy stated clear goals, and they were met, there would be no need for further activism.* And if its goals were not met, then those intent on a particular outcome could become discouraged. By making the self-authorizing practice of democracy the end of political action, Occupy may instead encourage the cultivation of democracy sense among participants that could energize and re-energize the movement for years to come, or outlive it should it fade.[50]

For Ferguson, it is actually a bad thing for a movement to achieve its goals, because the movement then has nothing left to do. This is the paradox of solving social problems: if a political actor gets everything she wants, then she has lost her reason for being a political actor.[51] If she cares more about being a political actor than anything else, then solving social problems actually interferes with what she wants in life. Her chosen means of gaining status through political grandstanding would disappear.

The paradox arises both at the level of individuals and at the level of organizations. For the individual, her identity as an activist and reformer is at stake. If she were to achieve all of her goals, she would have no reason to remain active in her cause, aside from watching vigilantly for a reappearance of the problems that once moved her. She could find a new cause, but it could take a lot of time and effort to regain similar status among activists who focus on different issues. We can agree that it is sometimes a sad fact of life that projects wind down. Meaningful relationships that were based around a common purpose can end. Until something else that matters to you comes along, you can feel lost. There is a natural tendency to want to linger and reminisce over past victories. But surely these regrets have little purchase when weighed against the possibility of solving a social problem important enough to devote oneself to. We have a hard time imagining many mature adults even verbalizing these thoughts, even though we think it is understandable to have them. Injustice is not an opportunity to show off for your friends or feel important. It is a call to make things right.

Organizations also face a version of the paradox. If an organization is established to solve a problem, and that problem then goes away, people could be out of a job. They might have moved, bought houses, started families, and organized their lives in other ways around the continued existence of that organization. Solving the problem could throw their lives into disarray. But again, that does not seem like a good reason to hope that the problem is not resolved, or to insist that something is still wrong when it is not. Perhaps the idea is that there is an advantage to keeping a group constituted so that it can respond quickly to sudden backsliding on the progress it has made. But surely it is possible to establish a

smaller standing organization based on response rather than proac-
tive engagement without turning your movement into the political
equivalent of an aimless temper tantrum.

Furthermore, due to the personal and group incentives for
activists to continue in their roles, there is pressure to moralize: to seek
ever more applications of morality to heal the world. There are many
wrongs in the world, no doubt. But there should also be no doubt
that many activists, seeking to continue their work to meet vague and
open-ended goals, find it irresistible to hunt for moral wrongs.

Consider Barrett Wilson, a self-described former "self-righteous
social justice crusader" who "once had a well paid job in what might
be described as the social justice industry."[52] In other words, he was
an activist. He lost his job when he himself was targeted by his very
own social justice mob. What interests us here is Wilson's confession
of the ever-expanding target of the activist's suspicious moral eye:

> Just a few years ago, many of my friends and peers who self-
> identify as liberals or progressives were open fans of provoca-
> tive standup comedians such as Sarah Silverman, and shows like
> South Park. Today, such material is seen as deeply "problematic,"
> or even labeled as hate speech. I went from minding my own
> business when people told risqué jokes to practically fainting
> when they used the wrong pronoun or expressed a right-of-
> center view. I went from making fun of the guy who took edgy
> jokes too seriously, to becoming that guy.

What's worse is that the very qualities that activists tend to
pride themselves on—militancy, hostility, unconventionality,
eccentricity—are the qualities that keep people from being recep-
tive to activists and their proposed changes. Psychologist Nadia
Bashir and colleagues conducted several studies, showing that

seemingly zealous dedication to a social cause may backfire and elicit unfavourable reactions from others. Indeed, individuals avoid affiliating with "typical" activists and adopting the pro-change behaviours that these activists advocate because individuals associate them with negative stereotypes. Ironically and despite good intentions, therefore, the very individuals who are most actively engaged in promoting social change may inadvertently alienate members of the public and reduce pro-change motivation.[53]

Grandstanding activists who make a show of their moral superiority in shaming or other kinds of hostile treatment may be doing more harm than good. The lesson here is clear: if we want to bring about actual social change in the world, we will advance that goal more effectively by not grandstanding about it.

Now that we've identified three dangers of political grandstanding, we should offer the other side some time. Are there any positive consequences of political grandstanding?

BENEFITS OF POLITICAL GRANDSTANDING?

In chapter 4, we identified two potential social benefits of grandstanding: it signals cooperation and motivates productive social action. In addition to these benefits, political grandstanding may produce another: it gives voters useful information. Knowing about a politician's values can be a useful heuristic for voters who do not have time to read about their policy positions or voting records. If you simply want to vote for the candidate who cares most about the poor or free trade, it would be useful for the various candidates to display such values. So if politicians were to stop grandstanding, such voters would be cut off from important information.

For this reason, we suspect that politicians are sometimes in situations where grandstanding is a permissible thing to do. Of course, the fact that political grandstanding can achieve some good is consistent with it still being bad for other reasons. It may still have other bad consequences, be disrespectful, or reveal a lack of virtue. At the end of the day, though, grandstanding might sometimes be permissible. If that's right, politicians may have greater license to grandstand than the rest of us do. The information-sharing function of political grandstanding could have an important role to play in a democracy.

It is important to keep in mind, however, that a politician's grandstanding will not always (and perhaps not often) communicate to voters something true about her moral qualities. Not every politician who grandstands to suggest she cares most about a value actually cares most about it. Some might not care at all, and they might even plan to ignore it. So the proposed informational benefit of political grandstanding can't just be that you learn something about the politician's character. Often the politician will give you bad information about her character.

Even if there is a valuable information-providing function of political grandstanding, you might worry about the following scenario. Suppose there are two political parties: the Evil Party and the Justice Party. Politicians from both parties grandstand to let potential voters know where their values lie. Because the Evil Party is just wrong about everything, wouldn't it be wrong all things considered for their politicians to grandstand, but permissible for those of the Justice Party?

It is important to keep in mind, however, that the defense of grandstanding we've been discussing is not that it helps voters vote for the politician who would do more good. Rather, what political grandstanding might do is help people vote according to their preferences. One of the core values of democratic governance is in making people feel at home in the world—ruled by their own choices that reflect their own values.[54] Helping people vote in a way that is true to their preferences matters to some degree, even if other things might matter more.

CONCLUSION

Grandstanding does significant damage to politics in a democracy. When people treat political discourse as a forum for self-aggrandizement, their interests frequently conflict with the goal of resolving social problems. Instead of compromising with the out-group, grandstanders attack its members, and describe their beliefs and policy proposals in bad faith. For in-group members who would be willing to compromise, grandstanders question their integrity and encourage others to shun them. Rather than promote dull policies that make a difference in complicated ways, grandstanders prefer the big splash that accomplishes little but allows them to claim credit for their effort. And for grandstanders who enjoy their current roles a bit too much, there is incentive not to undercut their reason for being by solving social problems.

Whether these bad effects (and the other problems we've identified) are enough to outweigh the good that political grandstanding can do is at least partly an empirical question to which we do not have a definitive answer. We suspect that on balance, grandstanding does more harm than good to our political process and its institutions. At any rate, we should not cheer wholeheartedly when politics becomes a morality pageant.

Chapter 8

What to Do About Grandstanding

We've now evaluated the morality of grandstanding, and concluded that it is bad behavior that we would do well to avoid. More than diagnosing it as a problem, we want to help readers think through solutions. How can we improve public moral discourse? Realistically, we can't aim to get rid of grandstanding entirely. We can try to reduce it significantly, however—and for all the reasons we've provided throughout this book, we should do so.

So how can we do this? How can we cut down on preening and posturing moral talk and all the damage it causes? To be honest, we're not sure. How do you get millions of people from all walks of life to stop using moral talk to satisfy the common human desire for social status? To compound the problem, it is difficult to know when people are grandstanding. No one can read minds and be certain of others' motivations. This makes grandstanding hard to monitor. Spotting grandstanders is not like issuing speeding tickets. Furthermore, due to our contentious political climate, giving *any* advice about how people should contribute to moral and political discourse is fraught with risks. Many people may have a difficult time taking such advice at face value and not as a kind of veiled attack on political enemies.

We're going to offer the best advice we can muster about how to tackle the problem of grandstanding. We must stress, though, that most of what we say is exploratory. We offer several empirically supported strategies that we think are promising means of reducing grandstanding. But we are eager to see future work from experts in other fields about how to infuse more modesty into our public discourse.

AGAINST CALLING OUT

One way to try to change people's behavior is to scold them. There is a common human impulse to tell people when they mess up. That might seem like an obvious way to address grandstanding: when you think you see someone grandstanding, call them out on it.

> BEN: Wells Fargo has once again shown contempt for its customers' privacy. Like others who care deeply about consumer rights and despise corporate greed, I am very strongly considering moving my checking account to another bank.
>
> ANN: "Very strongly considering?" Watch out everybody, man on fire! Stop with the grandstanding.

Many readers have probably felt the urge to say something like this. But in our view, calling out grandstanders is generally a bad strategy for improving public discourse.

To call someone out is to accuse her publicly of bad behavior. Leveling such an accusation requires justification. It would be unfair to go around wildly accusing someone of cheating on his partner, or of embezzling from his employer. At the very least, an accuser needs to be justifiably confident that her accusations are true. The costs of wrongfully accusing someone are often significant. Not only is it unjust, it could also seriously harm the target's reputation—possibly even ruining her life. The point is simple: to make a public accusation of bad behavior, you should be justifiably confident that your charge is accurate.

Sometimes this is an easy requirement to meet, like when a drunk celebrity is caught on camera using a racial slur. But sometimes the features of an action that make it wrong are hidden from plain view. Take lying, for example. It is difficult to know when someone is lying to your face. It is even harder to know whether someone is trying to deceive you simply from a written statement. Try it:

"Warmke avoids gluten."
"Tosi has seen Interpol in concert five times."

Studies show that, on average, people successfully detect lies at about a 54 percent rate.[1] Slightly better than the flip of a coin. Most of these studies allow the "detectors" to see the "liars'" facial expressions, but the detectors are not provided much additional context. Imagine how much harder it is to detect lies if all you have is a bit of text written by a stranger.

Here again, grandstanding has something in common with lying. Recall that grandstanders use moral talk to impress others with their supposed moral qualities. But it is difficult to know whether someone is contributing to public discourse for this reason, especially if the only evidence you have is a bit of written communication. To accuse someone of grandstanding, you should be justifiably confident that she is grandstanding. Yet since you usually don't know enough about what is motivating someone's moral talk, you usually aren't justified in publicly accusing her of grandstanding. This is a good reason not to call people out for grandstanding.

Let's pause for a moment to forestall a misunderstanding. We have claimed throughout the book that moral grandstanding is common in public discourse. Yet we just admitted that it is hard to know whether someone is grandstanding in particular cases. But how could we know that grandstanding is common if it's so hard to tell whether someone is grandstanding?

Suppose that every time you strongly suspect someone is grandstanding, there's a 50 percent chance you're right. (You don't know this about yourself, but let's assume for the moment that it's true.) Suppose you spend an hour on a social media site and see 100 posts that you strongly suspect of grandstanding. Convinced by our argument that it's hard to tell whether someone is grandstanding, you realize that you shouldn't be confident that any particular case is an instance of grandstanding. And yet it would very surprising if you had not seen dozens of cases of grandstanding in that hour.

Think once again about lying. As we've noted, it's often hard to know whether someone is lying to you. But it would be a mistake to conclude from that fact alone that there isn't much lying in the world. This is probably obvious to you without having to do research on the prevalence of lying. But people have studied such things and we know that lying is common in social life.[2]

So even if it's difficult to be sure about any given case of grandstanding, that doesn't mean we can't know whether grandstanding is common. Given that most of us are moral self-enhancers, and that we try to manage our impressions so that people think highly of us, it would be surprising if grandstanding were not common. In fact, our preliminary empirical research suggests that prestige-seeking grandstanding in particular is fairly common.[3] Even so, the fact that grandstanding is so often hard to detect is a good reason to resist the temptation to publicly accuse someone of doing it.

But what if you are justifiably confident that someone is grandstanding? Is it okay in these cases to call him out? Even here, your justified confidence doesn't necessarily mean it's okay to issue a public accusation. Accuracy alone doesn't license the making of accusations. Suppose your friend tells a corny joke at a dinner party. Even if you know the joke was bad, that doesn't make it okay to announce to the whole table what a terrible joke it was. That would be needlessly mean, not to mention a disproportionate response.

Similarly, even if someone really is grandstanding, calling her out in public is typically a poor response because it will be counterproductive. Once accusations of grandstanding are made, the ensuing discussion (if there is one at all) is usually nasty and unhelpful. Few of us, upon being publicly accused of grandstanding, have the self-control to keep from fighting back. So if you do accuse someone of grandstanding, the charge will likely just be turned around on you.[4] Or you'll be accused of silencing people.[5] Or you'll be criticized for not recognizing people's sincere concerns.[6] Or they'll say you're trying to inject your politics into the discussion.[7] Your accusation might even become the occasion for more grandstanding from others.

Accusations of grandstanding also tend to be counter-productive because the accused party can fall back on unverifiable claims about what she was trying to do. When someone accuses you of grandstanding, there is a simple response available: "I *was not* trying to impress people!" Then everyone can argue about the accuser's assessment of your motives versus your own. The next time such an argument is productive will also be the first time.

Still another problem with accusations of grandstanding is that conceptual drift quickly sets in with terms like "grandstanding." Conceptual drift occurs when the boundaries of a concept expand from what was once a clear idea to cover tangentially related phenomena.[8] Consider "mansplaining." In its early existence, the term was generally used to refer to a man giving a condescending and usually inaccurate explanation to a woman, often of something the woman understands better than the man.[9] The charge struck a popular chord, the term became popular, and soon enough it was being used to describe men talking in virtually any context. Once people see how useful it can be to apply a concept like mansplaining in more cases, they expand the range of things that qualify as mansplaining. For example, during a Question Time session in the House of Commons in 2017, Britain's Labour Party Leader, Jeremy Corbyn, said, "Tomorrow is International Women's Day, a chance to both celebrate how far we've come on equality for women, but also to reflect on how far we have to go, not just in this country but around the world." To which British Prime Minister Theresa May replied, "Well, first of all, can I thank the right honorable gentleman for telling me that it is International Women's Day tomorrow? I think that's what's called 'mansplaining.'"[10]

When used frequently as a public condemnation, the term "grandstanding" might fall prey to the same kind of drift. Terms that are hard to define and behavior that is difficult to identify are especially liable to drift. The path is a predictable one. People discover that they can use charges of grandstanding to dismiss a speaker without substantive engagement. Next thing you know, people will be using the term against anyone who makes them ideologically uncomfortable.

We can imagine someone saying: "You've just argued against calling out grandstanders. And yet you've written a whole book criticizing grandstanding. Isn't that hypocritical? Shouldn't you be taking your own advice?"

There are two ways to publicly criticize grandstanding. First, you can publicly accuse a particular person of grandstanding. You might make the accusation directly to the person (as a response on social media, say). Or you might publicly accuse someone without her knowing (like denouncing a grandstanding politician on Twitter). These are *personal* criticisms.

But a second kind of public criticism involves negatively assessing grandstanding in general. Such criticisms are not accusations against any particular person. These are *general* criticisms. Just like you can say lying is bad without calling out any particular person for lying, you can say grandstanding is bad without calling out individual grandstanders. We caution against personal criticism of grandstanders, but that doesn't preclude general criticism of grandstanding.

Morality rarely gives us hard and fast rules about difficult situations in life. But it seems to us that, in general, public accusations of grandstanding will make things worse. Further, once people see the potency of personal criticism for grandstanding, many will want to wield this power over others by condemning them for any moral talk at all, which is a terrible outcome. For these reasons, we recommend against calling out grandstanders.

For many readers, calling grandstanders out will seem like the only possible response. Without this weapon in our arsenal, the prospect of minimizing grandstanding might seem like a lost cause. But don't despair. We have some other ideas about how to reduce grandstanding and improve moral talk.

PERSONAL CHANGE

Many of us have settled into bad habits in our use of moral talk. Some may even be serial grandstanders. Others may dabble occasionally when the urge is too strong to resist. If we're honest with ourselves, we can all admit to grandstanding, or at least to feeling tempted to do so.

Human beings have limited willpower. Even when our sincere moral convictions recommend against doing bad things, we do not automatically do what is right. As the old joke goes, we can resist everything except temptation.[11] People who have tried to stop smoking will understand. So will married people who remain incorrigible flirts. Perhaps grandstanding is similarly tempting. Belief in one's own moral superiority is common. Our desire for approval from others may also be hard to keep at bay.

But grandstanding is not an inevitable feature of public discourse. We might have strong desires that others hold us in high moral esteem, but that doesn't necessarily mean it's okay to act on them. Having a strong desire for flirtatious attention doesn't make it okay to flirt with colleagues. Wanting to be admired doesn't make it okay to dominate dinner conversation with boasts of your accomplishments. By the time we reach adulthood, most of us have learned not to engage in these anti-social behaviors. We can learn self-restraint when it comes to grandstanding, too. There are various personal changes you can make to cut down on your own grandstanding. Notice that we say cut down on, rather than eliminate. Personal change is difficult. Even if you try your hardest, you will probably still fall short. But that's okay. Even if you don't manage to stop grandstanding altogether, you should be happy if you manage to grandstand less.

Engineer Your Situations

One of the best-supported discoveries in psychology in the twentieth century was that situations play a major role in shaping our behavior. For instance, in one experiment, participants were tested to see whether they would help someone in the next room upon hearing a loud crash and screaming. Seventy percent of those who were alone during the incident helped. But when paired with a confederate who reacted to the noise with indifference, only 7 percent helped.[12] In another study, participants were twice as likely to help deliver some documents 40 meters away if they were asked to do so right after leaving a public bathroom.[13]

"Situationism" is a theory that says situations exert a powerful influence in shaping our behavior.[14] You recognize this fact implicitly when you take care to avoid enticement. While you are trying to quit smoking, you don't take the route home that passes your favorite cigar shop, for instance.

Changes in your situation can also help you improve your behavior in public discourse. You might think you can peruse Twitter for hours a day and not get angry enough to shoot off a self-righteous, grandstanding tweet. You might think you can avoid posting an incendiary and exaggerated claim on Facebook, despite knowing that it will receive universal acclaim from your like-minded friends. But for many of us, the temptation will be too strong to resist. It is often better to avoid these tempting situations altogether. Here are some suggestions:

- Limit the time you spend on social media. One of our best-behaved academic friends allows himself 30 minutes a day. You might install an app on your phone such as App Detox, Off the Grid, or Antisocial that can block or limit your access to social media.
- When using social media, try muting or unfollowing those who are reckless and intemperate when discussing politics. Seeing this kind of behavior—especially from those on the "other side"—is a recipe for temptation to grandstand.

Experiment with a "three-strikes" rule: if someone angers or annoys you three times, unfollow them.

- Consider avoiding extremely partisan news sources that get you worked up about the other side. Or try limiting yourself to, say, no more than one hour of Rachel Maddow or Sean Hannity a week.

Plan to Succeed

Work out more. Consume less sugar. Read more good books. With few exceptions, we fail at these goals. Why? In the 1990s, psychologist Peter Gollwitzer put a finger on the problem: we have no plan.

Gollwitzer introduced the term "implementation intention" to refer to our plans for accomplishing our goals. When we form implementation intentions, we decide when, where, and how we intend to pursue our goals. Suppose your goal is to stop smoking. You could form an implementation intention by deciding to go to the store on Wednesday nights to buy nicotine gum. Or you could decide that you'll go for a walk whenever you feel the urge to smoke.

Implementation intentions can help people reach difficult goals. Consider one study of drug addicts experiencing withdrawal. Two groups of addicts were tasked with writing a short résumé before 5 p.m. This was their goal. One of the groups was also told to write out specifics as to how and when they would complete their task. The second group formed no such implementation intentions. Although no one in the second group wrote a résumé, 80 percent of those in the implementation group did. Similar results have been discovered for many other kinds of goals, such as getting a mammogram, losing weight, and eating more vegetables.[15] There is also evidence that implementation intentions can help us regulate our emotions.[16]

For those who want to improve their moral talk, implementation intentions might help. Such intentions are particularly helpful when we face strong temptation in the heat of the moment. When you're frustrated or outraged about what people are saying or doing online, previously formed implementation intentions can help guide your behavior by giving you a plan to fall back on. Restraint will thus be easier for you. Here are some suggestions for the kinds of intentions you might form. We'll word them as if-then statements, because that's when they're most effective.[17]

- If I see a political post that makes me angry, I will open a new browser tab and read about sports/watch Netflix/reply to an email/do anything non-politics related.
- If I see someone say something stupid or uninformed, I will not rush to correct them.
- If I say something mean or narcissistic to someone online about morality or politics, I will apologize to them publicly for it.

Redirect Your Recognition Desire

For many of us, wanting others to be impressed with our moral credentials is a strong and natural desire. We suggested some ways to restrain this desire and avoid grandstanding. It can also be helpful to find other productive outlets to satisfy the Recognition Desire.

Public moral discourse is not the appropriate venue for seeking prestige. There are better ways to get people to think you are morally impressive—ways that have better consequences, treat others with respect, and help you to be a more virtuous person. Those options are obviously morally preferable. Luckily, they also aren't difficult to find. We won't instruct you on what to do with your time, but with a little searching, you can find organizations in your community that could use volunteers to help them do some good. The people there will likely be grateful for whatever you can contribute. Or you could just look around more informally for people close to you who could use some goodwill. Unlike moral grandstanding, even if you're doing good because you want to impress others, you'll probably still be doing something positive overall.

Although changing our own behavior is the safest approach to combating grandstanding, there is only so much you can do to reduce grandstanding simply by limiting your own. We also need some means of discouraging grandstanding from others. So we turn next to some suggestions for spurring broader social change.

SOCIAL CHANGE

Imagine that your community practices open defecation. People just dump their feces into a river, the banks of which your community calls home. This has resulted in unhealthy drinking water, a high infant mortality rate, and delayed childhood development due to illness. It's easier to use the river instead of disposing of your waste properly. Once you've become aware of how unhealthy open defecation is and how much harm it causes, though, you might decide to stop defecating in the river. However, the rest of your community does not follow suit. They keep using the river as a communal latrine. If you are the only one who stops dumping your feces in the river, you will still be affected by others' waste, as of course will they. What you need to do is to get them to stop dumping, too.

Many people treat public discourse like that river, indiscriminately spewing their own brand of waste. You might avoid grandstanding yourself, but if others still pollute public discourse with their own grandstanding, you will still have to deal with the consequences. We need to find a way to help others stop grandstanding, too.

Most modern cultures have a social norm against open defecation. Members of those cultures believe that other members are not practicing open defecation. They also know that there is a general belief that members *shouldn't* practice open defecation. However, some regions, particularly the rural areas of India, still have high rates of open defecation. The problem isn't poverty: India has a higher open defecation rate than much poorer countries. Nor is the problem lack of infrastructure: for decades, India has built latrines in rural areas to combat open defecation. Rather, the problem is with social norms supported by the caste system. Emptying latrines—the only technology available for disposing of human waste—is regarded as Dalit (untouchable) work. Non-Dalits won't do it. Dalits also generally avoid it, fearing ostracism. So in the absence of a better solution, people resort to open defecation, and it is regarded as normal.[18]

India's open defecation problem has drawn the attention of social scientists because it raises a difficult puzzle: how do you get a culture to change a social norm? Philosopher Cristina Bicchieri has taken up precisely this question, setting out a detailed strategy for replacing bad social norms with better ones.[19] Taking cues from Bicchieri's approach to changing norms, we'll offer a strategy for turning the tide against grandstanding and toward a more effective and respectful public discourse. Fundamentally, we want to go from something like:

Current Norm: Many people grandstand, think it's okay to grandstand, and are rewarded for grandstanding.

To something like:

> *New Norm*: Few people grandstand or think it's okay to grand-
> stand. When they do, they are not rewarded for it.

Borrowing from Bicchieri, we propose a three-step process to help us think about how to change the culture around grandstanding.

Step 1: Correcting Beliefs

If you want people to stop defecating in public, the first thing to do is to teach them how toxic their waste is, and how they can most effectively get rid of it.[20] It's not obvious. This must be explained.

The first step in changing a social norm is to correct peoples' beliefs. Specifically, we want to change both factual beliefs and personal normative beliefs.

Factual beliefs are your beliefs about the way things are. To reform the culture of grandstanding, we need to help others change some of their beliefs. First, most of us need to change certain beliefs about ourselves. People have mistaken beliefs about how morally enlightened they are. We are moral self-enhancers who exaggerate our moral qualities. Second, we also have mistaken factual beliefs about others. We overestimate the extent to which others need or want to hear about how morally good we are. And we think our grandstanding is much more successful in impressing others than it actually is. Third, we have mistaken beliefs about the effects of our contributions to public discourse. Grandstanders take too rosy a view of the consequences of their behavior.

In addition to false factual beliefs, grandstanders also tend to have false personal normative beliefs. These are beliefs about what you should or shouldn't do. For example, grandstanders think they should use moral talk to show off their moral qualities (or at least that it's okay to do so). They think they should use outrage or shaming to silence people who aren't as morally good as they are. But they are mistaken about this.

You can think of this book as an attempt at this first step. It is one long argument for why we should think differently about moral talk. If you've read this far, you now know more about the nature and pitfalls of moral grandstanding than most people, and you are well-equipped to explain to interested friends what is going wrong in public discourse. But you're only one person, and you shouldn't try to do too much. In addition to your own work, let us help—this book would make a wonderful gift for your friends and family this political season.

Step 2: Set a Good Example

Many people who treat public discourse as their own personal waste disposal site probably don't know any better. Even if they do know better, they may not have had many experiences with healthy public discourse. Many who have grown up on social media think that much of what they see just is what moral talk looks like. Imbibing years of partisan media can affect your views about what qualifies as good moral talk. For some, exchanging sick burns on Twitter *just is* what it means to talk politics. What many people need is simply to be shown a better way.

In their book *Why We Argue (and How We Should)*, philosophers Scott Aiken and Robert Talisse discuss the many ways in which political disagreement can go wrong and offer several suggestions for how to improve our own contributions to public discourse.[21] A few of their strategies might help you avoid grandstanding. For starters, Aiken and Talisse suggest that we avoid treating every issue as a simple problem with a simple solution. When discussing morality and politics, it's okay to admit that many problems are complicated and that solutions are not obvious to anyone who is not morally corrupt. Additionally, they suggest that, when you argue, you should make your premises clear. As we have discussed in this book, much moral grandstanding involves trying to shut someone down by being outraged or expressing shock and being dismissive. But outrage and shock are not arguments or reasons. As Aiken and Talisse point out, it is fallacious to make the leap from "I am outraged by the things Sam said" to "Therefore, Sam is wrong." If you think someone is wrong, try to articulate what your reasoning is for rejecting what he says.

Lastly, Aiken and Talisse encourage us to admit when we realize we are wrong or that someone else has made a good point in conversation. What are the odds that you are right about everything you think and say? Productive conversations are more likely to happen when we admit our mistakes. Digging in may help you save face, but it's not a recipe for productive disagreement about our differences.

We have one final suggestion of our own. When you engage in moral talk, be harder on yourself than you are on others. Many of us have a tendency to criticize others more than we do ourselves. This is not surprising. We rate others against the set of idiosyncratic moral criteria to which we hold ourselves. Naturally, others will do worse according to a set of moral standards they aren't even aware of. Furthermore, although we tend to attribute our own failings to our bad luck or circumstances beyond our control ("I missed the red light because the sun got in my eye"), we tend to attribute others' failings to their bad character ("She missed the red light because she's a reckless driver").[22] But this is unfair. To counteract our biases, we should be prepared to give others the benefit of the doubt. As philosopher Robert Fullinwider puts it, "morality imposes a basic division of labor: it requires from us charity towards others and strictness with ourselves."[23]

The point of setting an example is, of course, not to show that you are better than others. Rather, as Bicchieri explains, "informing people about the efficacy of a behavior is not nearly as convincing as showing them examples of individuals who successfully practice it."[24] This might mean setting your own good example. If other people see that there's a better way of talking about moral matters, they might just recognize it, and respond in kind.

Step 3: Sanction Grandstanders

If we want people to stop doing something—like publicly defecating or grandstanding—we should also introduce sanctions for non-compliance. The goal is for people to know that the response to their grandstanding will be unpleasant. We have argued that calling out grandstanders is probably a bad idea. But there are other forms of sanction that could work better, by making it unpleasant for people to grandstand. Here are a couple of tentative suggestions.

One way to make it unpleasant to grandstand is to make grandstanding embarrassing. You can do your part in accomplishing this goal by being withholding. On social media, you can withhold your praise, your Facebook likes, your Twitter retweets. No more "This is amazingly brave" comments for people who take costless stands defending their moral convictions that are obvious crowd-pleasers directed at their like-minded friends. Don't support politicians just because they come across as one of the good guys in publicity stunts. When people engage in self-righteous displays at work, ignore them. The basic idea is not to give people credit for their attention-seeking.

Imagine, for example, crafting a carefully worded Facebook post detailing all the nuances of your utter disgust at the local university for serving culturally appropriated Chinese food in the dining hall, only to be met with zero likes. What the authors of such posts want is the very thing they shouldn't get: your praise. If more of us withheld our praise for grandstanding, it might become clearer that it doesn't pay.

We claimed earlier that it is a bad idea to call out or shame grandstanders because it is usually difficult to know whether someone is grandstanding. You might worry that our suggestion to be withholding conflicts with this claim. If we don't know enough to call out and shame alleged grandstanders, how could we know enough to withhold praise?

There is a crucial difference, however, between calling people out and withholding praise. When you call people out for grandstanding, you publicly criticize them. If you are wrong, you might unfairly damage their reputation. And even if you are right and they deserve the criticism, calling them out will still probably lead to an unhelpful discussion about whether they really are grandstanding. You'll also likely be accused of trying to silence or tone police others. The stakes are high when you are considering whether to call someone out.

But the stakes are much lower when withholding praise. If you're right that someone is grandstanding, you succeed in not rewarding someone who doesn't deserve to be rewarded. But if you are wrong and withhold praise, what is lost? Not much more than what would be lost by not being on social media at all. (In fact, by doing this you might find yourself with enough free time to do something much more meaningful and rewarding, like the volunteering or other involvement we suggested as an alternative way for grandstanders to channel their energies.) Even truly courageous or insightful non-grandstanding social media posts don't require your attention and support. Because much less is at stake, it's okay to withhold praise for cases of suspected grandstanding even when it would not be okay to call the same person out.

Our second suggestion for sanctioning grandstanders is more aggressive, and we offer it with some reservations. But here it is: when you see someone using grandstanding for cover—that is, to make people less suspicious that they are the kind of person who does the bad things they do, as we discussed previously—consider calling him out publicly for the bad behavior he is trying to cover up. Obviously, this should not be done lightly. You should not accuse someone of wrongdoing unless you have convincing evidence for that accusation. And it might not be your place to level the accusation anyway, given that the grandstander's victims might have good reason not to want the details of their lives dragged into the public eye. But grandstanding for cover is a dangerous phenomenon. Many people are taken in by these grandstanders' acts, and, as a result, grandstanders are often free to continue wronging others.

Few things make us angry about grandstanding anymore. But we still feel frustration when we hear people say they can't believe some celebrity or public figure would ever hurt a woman, abuse a child, or whatever else because he frequently pays lip service to their favored values. Tell the victims of Harvey Weinstein, Roy Moore, and other talented grandstanders that a little grandstanding never hurt anyone. If you see a sorry act like theirs at work, don't accuse the perpetrator of grandstanding. Accuse him of the wrongdoing his grandstanding is designed to cover up.

When enough people start treating discourse differently, norms can change. Many people who come to see why it is bad to abuse moral talk will stop grandstanding. They will realize they are mistreating others and ruining a public resource. They will notice that in the long run, grandstanding often backfires—temptations to grandstand promise much but deliver little. They will recognize the prospects of a better discourse and set a good example. And they will take it upon themselves to withhold from still-practicing grandstanders the very thing they desire: the praise of others. Once enough people learn about the dangers of grandstanding and see that it is often met with silence, it will become embarrassing to indulge our desires for praise in the public square.

A REASON FOR OPTIMISM

You might be forgiven for reading our remarks about changing norms about grandstanding and rolling your eyes. We're so far from a world in which grandstanding is thought of as a serious norm violation that our advice might sound quaint. How could we ever think things could change so much?

It's not easy to change norms. Nor is the process quick. It might seem impossible to get so many people to stop treating public discourse as their vanity project. But when enough people start treating discourse differently, norms can change. Norms change all the time, for better and for worse, even when the behavior they regulate seems deeply ingrained in human nature.

Consider, for example, another kind of norm: table manners. Here are some common pieces of advice for proper table behavior in polite company, taken from Medieval and Renaissance-era etiquette manuals:

- "It is unseemly to blow your nose into the tablecloth."[25]
- Do not "fall upon the dishes like swine while eating, snorting disgustingly and smacking [your] lips."[26]

- It is a "serious offense" to "gnaw a bone and then put it back in the [serving] dish."[27]
- And Erasmus, in a colorful passage, notes disapprovingly that some "devour rather than eat, as if they were about to be carried off to prison," or "push so much into their mouths that their cheeks bulge like bellows." And others "pull their lips apart while eating, so that they make a noise like pigs."[28]

Perhaps it will be difficult for readers to imagine that these things were written for adults living in a civilized society. But that is actually encouraging. Think about it this way. This messy behavior must have been widespread enough to justify the use of paper and ink to warn against it. Further, this behavior must have seemed to many like a natural and efficient way of satisfying basic human desires. And yet it has become nearly unthinkable for us to encounter someone doing any of these things in public. Instead of everyone blowing their noses into the tablecloth, we somehow arrived at a point where this behavior is embarrassing. How did we get to this point? By the promotion of different social norms, people came to think of these and other violations of etiquette as embarrassing.

The success of these norm changes should be encouraging to those of us who are currently worried about grandstanding. Grandstanding, too, is widespread, and many people accept it as a natural and efficient way of satisfying a basic human desire for recognition. Though it might seem unrealistic from where we stand now, we can change how we behave in public moral discourse, and we should.

NOTES

Preface

1. https://quillette.com/2018/07/14/i-was-the-mob-until-the-mob-came-for-me/ [accessed 9/15/18]

Chapter 1

1. Each of these behaviors is a warning sign of narcissistic personality disorder in children. https://www.psychologytoday.com/blog/warning-signs-parents/201701/childhood-roots-narcissistic-personality-disorder [accessed 7/8/18]
2. http://www.oxygen.com/very-real/woman-was-destroyed-on-twitter-for-blaming-white-mens-entitlement-for-alligator-death [accessed 7/8/18]
3. https://twitter.com/TheBrandonMorse/status/914885815901319168 [accessed 7/8/18]
4. Sarkeesian has archived the abusive Tweets here: https://femfreq.tumblr.com/post/109319269825/one-week-of-harassment-on-twitter [accessed 7/8/18].
5. https://www.bbc.com/news/av/world-us-canada-24308586/obama-attacks-republican-grandstanding [accessed 7/7/18]
6. http://www.latimes.com/opinion/editorials/la-ed-planned-parenthood-senate-vote-20150804-story.html [accessed 7/7/18]
7. https://www.brookings.edu/blog/up-front/2012/10/09/mitt-romneys-foreign-policy-agenda/ [accessed 7/7/18]

8. https://www.nytimes.com/2017/10/18/opinion/whats-the-matter-with-republicans.html [accessed 7/7/18]
9. http://www.donaldjtrump.com/positions/second-amendment-rights [accessed 1/6/16]
10. https://www.nbcnews.com/news/us-news/trump-reveals-he-asked-comey-whether-he-was-under-investigation-n757821 [accessed 7/7/18]
11. https://www.washingtonpost.com/news/the-fix/wp/2018/06/26/trump-cant-stop-dissing-john-mccain/ [accessed 7/7/18]
12. http://money.cnn.com/2017/10/05/media/harvey-weinsteins-full-statement/ [accessed 7/8/18]
13. https://www.theatlantic.com/politics/archive/2017/09/the-lawlessness-of-roy-moore/541467/ [accessed 4/28/19]
14. https://www.washingtonpost.com/news/powerpost/wp/2017/11/14/in-new-tv-ad-alabama-democrat-hits-roy-moore-over-awful-allegations/ [accessed 7/8/18]
15. http://www.nationalreview.com/corner/454230/philosophy-professor-makes-terrible-argument-roy-moore [accessed 7/8/18]
16. http://edition.cnn.com/TRANSCRIPTS/0308/14/se.03.html [accessed 6/26/18]

Chapter 2

1. (Kelly 1888)
2. http://www.thecrimson.com/article/1970/10/17/books-at-war-with-asia-313/ [accessed 7/8/18]
3. https://newrepublic.com/article/91139/indira-gandhi-corruption-india-supreme-court [accessed 7/8/18]
4. https://www.rogerebert.com/reviews/just-before-nightfall-1976 [accessed 7/8/18]
5. Philosophers and other academic readers might be interested in our fuller and more technical account of moral grandstanding as a prototype concept in (Tosi and Warmke 2016).
6. (Cheng, Tracy, and Henrich 2010; Henrich 2015)
7. (Buss and Dedden 1990; Schmitt and Buss 2001)
8. Our early results are summarized and discussed in a paper with psychologists Joshua B. Grubbs, A. Shanti James, and W. Keith Campbell, "Moral Grandstanding in Public Discourse: Status-seeking Motives as a Potential Explanatory Mechanism in Predicting Conflict" (2019), available here: https://psyarxiv.com/gnaj5/. All our data is available on the Open Science Framework here: https://osf.io/r3j45/.
9. (Grubbs et al. 2019)

10. (Leary and Kowalski 1990, 35)
11. (Grice 1989)
12. (Pinker, Nowak, and Lee 2008)
13. Inspired by (Wittels 2012, 71).
14. For brief discussion of the kinds of contextual features than can help or hinder impression management, see (Steinmetz, Sezer, and Sedikides 2017, 2–3). See also (Grice 1989).
15. On competence, see (Brown 2012; Möller and Savyon 2003). On ambition, see (Alicke et al. 2001). On intelligence, see (van Lange and Sedikides 1998). On wisdom, see (Zell and Alicke 2011).
16. (M. Ross and Sicoly 1979; Fields and Schuman 1976; T. W. Smith, Rasinski, and Toce 2001; White and Plous 1995)
17. (Cross 1977)
18. (Goethals, Messick, and Allison 1991)
19. (Tappin and McKay 2017)
20. (Epley and Dunning 2000; Fetchenhauer and Dunning 2006; Klein and Epley 2016, 2017)
21. (van Lange and Sedikides 1998)
22. (Tappin and McKay 2017; Dunning 2016)
23. See (Dunning 2016, 172).
24. (Klein and Epley 2016, 660). See also (Allison, Messick, and Goethals 1989; van Lange and Sedikides 1998; Epley and Dunning 2000; Sedikides and Alicke 2012).
25. (Goethals 1986)
26. (Epley and Dunning 2000)
27. (Klein and Epley 2017)
28. (Sedikides et al. 2014)
29. For a discussion of surveys of hundreds of thousands of people across the globe, see (McGrath 2015), who found "substantial cross-cultural convergence in the self-rating of character strengths" (McGrath 2015, 43).
30. (Liu 2013). Evidence suggests that people in collectivist cultures (like China) tend to morally self-enhance less than those in individualist cultures (United States, England) (Liu 2013; Dunning 2016). Yet even people in collectivist cultures self-enhance about their superior collectivist qualities (Sedikides, Gaertner, and Toguchi 2003; Sedikides, Gaertner, and Vevea 2005). In other words, cultural context changes how self-enhancement is expressed, but the general human tendency to self-enhance apparently runs deeper than culture.
31. (Tappin and McKay 2017)
32. (C. Miller 2017, 156)
33. (Epley and Dunning 2000)
34. (Epley and Dunning 2000)
35. (Tappin and McKay 2017)

36. (Leary and Kowalski 1990)
37. (Rom and Conway 2018)
38. (Vonasch et al. 2018)
39. (Leary and Kowalski 1990)
40. Psychologists call this pre-attentive impression management (Leary and Kowalski 1990).
41. (Nisbett and Wilson 1977)
42. https://aeon.co/ideas/confabulation-why-telling-ourselves-stories-makes-us-feel-ok [accessed 7/7/18]
43. (Simler and Hanson 2018, 105)
44. (von Hippel and Trivers 2011)
45. (Grice 1989)
46. (Goffman 1959, 13)
47. (Laurent et al. 2014; Powell and Smith 2013)
48. (Heck and Krueger 2016)
49. https://www.vanityfair.com/hollywood/2017/01/meryl-streep-donald-trump-golden-globes-speech [accessed 2/10/19]
50. https://twitter.com/Lavernecox/status/818295093564059648 [accessed 7/7/18]
51. https://twitter.com/unfoRETTAble/status/818295017152258048 [accessed 7/7/18]
52. https://twitter.com/MarkRonson/status/818292916787429377 [accessed 7/7/18]
53. https://www.nationalreview.com/2017/01/meryl-streep-golden-globes-speech-political-donald-trump-moralizing-hypocrisy/ [accessed 7/7/18]. Though not everyone who shares Streep's political views was impressed. See https://variety.com/2017/tv/news/trevor-noah-meryl-streep-speech-tone-deaf-1201956927/ [accessed 7/7/18]
54. https://www.nytimes.com/2017/08/08/magazine/virtue-signaling-isnt-the-problem-not-believing-one-another-is.html [accessed 7/8/18]
55. (Grubbs et al. 2019)
56. https://www.spectator.co.uk/2015/10/i-invented-virtue-signalling-now-its-taking-over-the-world/ [accessed 7/7/18]
57. (Zahavi 1975; Zahavi and Zahavi 1999)
58. (Jamie 2017)
59. (Caplan 2018)

Chapter 3

1. (Nozick 1990, 303)
2. No relation.
3. https://www.nytimes.com/2018/05/02/world/asia/chinese-prom-dress.html [accessed 7/17/18]

4. (Asch 1956)

5. Rod Bond and Peter Smith surveyed social scientific work on conformity covering 133 studies in 17 countries. They discovered that "conformity was significantly higher, (a) the larger the size of the majority, (b) the greater the proportion of female respondents, (c) when the majority did not consist of out-group members, and (d) the more ambiguous the stimulus" (Bond and Smith 1996, 124). But they also found that levels of conformity have declined since the original Asch studies, and that members of individualist cultures are less likely to conform than are members of collectivist cultures.

6. Amusingly, video recordings show participants exchanging what might fairly be described as loving glances with the other dissenter. See https://www.youtube.com/watch?v=TYIh4MkcfJA [accessed 7/17/18].

7. CELIMENE: He's *so* self-*satisfied!* —

   Yes, that's the word for *him*—what *monstrous* pride!
   His chief, his one, his *all-consuming* thought
   Is that he's not been "recognized" at *Court*
   Which he denounces all day, *every* day
   The "powers that be" ignore him—how dare they?
   It's a perpetual bilious tirade —
   No post's allotted, no appointment made
   That's not a "grave injustice" to the man.
   (Moliere 2008, 44)

8. (Willer, Kuwabara, and Macy 2009)

9. On the general phenomenon of "preference falsification," see (Kuran 1995).

10. (Willer, Kuwabara, and Macy 2009) did not test for the false enforcement of explicitly moral views. Is it possible that people would be more inclined to speak out against what they believe to be popular views if those views are moral ones—about, say, abortion or same-sex marriage? We doubt it, though we aren't aware of any studies that test specifically for this. There is evidence, however, that people strategically alter their moral judgments "in order to present situationally favorable impressions" (Rom and Conway 2018, 32).

11. (C. S. Ryan and Bogart 1997)

12. (Marques, Yzerbyt, and Leyens 1988; Pinto et al. 2010)

13. Of course, it is often difficult to know whether any given display of solidarity is laudable or instead an instance of grandstanding. It might be tempting to avoid this problem by claiming that all displays of solidarity are laudable. But reality is more complicated than that. For instance, after the Brexit vote, some in the United Kingdom took to wearing safety pins conspicuously on their clothing to signal their support for refugees and immigrants. The symbol reappeared briefly in the United States after the election of President Trump, when people used the pins to declare themselves allies of minority groups. Some pin-wearers probably did so out of genuine care for those groups, believing that

their members would find comfort in seeing their pin, and didn't care whether anyone else was impressed. Other pin-wearers likely felt proud of themselves and their friends for displaying their costless and insular signal of dissent from the recent election result as they went about their business largely in isolation from the disadvantaged people they claimed to be supporting. Indeed, some probably could not wait to post a photo of a pin on their social media adorned with the appropriate hashtags, just to get in on the action. We are grateful to Tamler Sommers and David Pizarro for this example.

14. (Norris and Kristensen 2006)

15. Cold war rhetoric was dominated by ill-founded speculation about various "gaps," which was so effectively mocked in Stanley Kubrick's 1964 film *Dr. Strangelove*. On the "missile gap," see (Preble 2003).

16. (Festinger 1954)

17. (Rom and Conway 2018)

18. The story is variously referred to as "The Real Princess," as it is in (Andersen 1993, 69). There is also an Italian story with a similar plot, usually translated as "The Most Sensitive Woman," collected in (Schneller 1867, 128–29). In that story, the prince decides to marry a woman whose foot was bandaged and immobilized after a breeze blew a petal from a jasmine blossom onto it.

19. http://insider.foxnews.com/2014/09/23/%E2%80%98how-disrespectful-was-that%E2%80%99-karl-rove-blasts-obama%E2%80%99s-%E2%80%98latte-salute%E2%80%99 [accessed 9/20/18]

20. https://www.breitbart.com/blog/2014/09/23/Obama-s-Disrespectful-Latte-Salute-Shocks-and-Offends/ [accessed 9/20/18]

21. (Driver 2005, 137)

22. Note that moralizing is not the same thing as grandstanding. Rather, grandstanding can be a form that moralizing takes. The older homeowner need not have been trying to impress anyone with his moral credentials. Yet some forms of grandstanding, such as trumping up, may involve moralizing.

23. (Mill 1989, 85)

24. (J. Jordan et al. 2017; Kennedy and Schweitzer 2015; Tetlock 2002)

25. The story about trust includes an interesting wrinkle. While observers raise their degree of *cognitive* trust in accusers—that is, they think of them as more reliable as reporters of the truth—they downgrade their assessment of accusers in terms of *affective* trust—as people with whom they might like to share some emotional bond. Accusers suffer lowered affective trust because making an accusation signals low benevolence. People regard accusers as more likely to subject them to an accusation, and so trust them less affectively (Kennedy and Schweitzer 2015).

26. https://newsroom.fb.com/company-info/ [accessed 7/17/18]

27. http://www.adweek.com/digital/data-never-sleeps/ [accessed 11/18/17]

28. http://files.shareholder.com/downloads/AMDA-2F526X/ 5458918398x0x961121/3D6E4631-9478-453F-A813-8DAB496307A1/ Q3_17_Shareholder_Letter.pdf [accessed 11/18/17]

29. https://www.omnicoreagency.com/twitter-statistics/ [accessed 11/18/17]

30. The authors found that "the right uses decidedly more outrage speech than the left," though the "worst individual offenders came from both the left and the right" (2014, 42). This was undoubtedly true in 2009, the first year of Barack Obama's presidency. We would be surprised, though, if the left has not overtaken the right in outrage rhetoric and anger as we write this in 2019, the third year of Donald Trump's presidency. A 2017 Pew Research Center study of Facebook found that "in response to posts from congressional Democrats, the proportion of reactions from the Facebook audience that used the "angry" button more than tripled after the [2016 Presidential] election." By contrast, angry reactions to Republican-shared news links remained "relatively stable." http://www.people-press.org/2017/12/18/sharing-the-news-in-a-polarized-congress/ [accessed 12/19/17]

31. (Berry and Sobieraj 2014, 36)

32. See, for example, (Skitka, Bauman, and Sargis 2005; Skitka 2010).

33. (Skitka 2010, 267)

34. This is so even when controlling for variables such as religiosity, attitude extremity, and political involvement. See (Skitka 2010; Mullen and Skitka 2006; Skitka and Wisneski 2011).

35. People also use their feelings of outrage to maintain feelings of self-righteousness (Green et al. 2019).

36. (Skitka and Wisneski 2011, 329)

37. While there is some evidence that the left and right emphasize different moral values (Haidt 2012), Skitka and colleagues have found little difference along ideological lines when it comes to moral conviction: "In summary, liberals and conservatives sometimes differ in the degree of moral conviction they attach to specific issues: conservatives, for example, are more morally convicted than liberals about the federal budget and deficit, immigration, and abortion, whereas liberals are more strongly convicted than conservatives about inequality, education, and the environment. Nonetheless, liberals and conservatives do not differ in their (1) overall levels of moral conviction collapsing across issues, (2) their levels of moral conviction for issues that are of most importance to them, or (3) tendency to moralize more rather than [fewer] issues (controlling for issue importance). People across the political spectrum are similar in their propensity to ground their positions in moral conviction" (Skitka, Morgan, and Wisneski 2015, 67).

38. (Rothschild and Keefer 2017)

39. (Rothschild and Keefer 2017)

40. (Green et al. 2019, 209)

41. From his 2012 Comedy Central special, *Standup Comedian*.

42. The main issue, according to one review of the evidence, is that polygraphs are designed to detect anxiety, which could be caused by all sorts of things unrelated to lying—like being subjected to uncomfortable questions in a strange setting (Saxe, Dougherty, and Cross 1985). For that matter, the tests can be defeated by subjects who take countermeasures such as pressing their toes on the floor, or counting backwards by 7 during questioning (Honts and Kircher 1994).

43. (Adelson 2004)

44. For more on this, see (Grubbs et al. 2019).

Chapter 4

1. https://www.youtube.com/watch?v=aFQFB5YpDZE [accessed 6/4/19]. In fairness we should point out that, fifteen years later, the late-night comedy landscape that Stewart helped shape has arguably lost the plot, too, delivering crowd-pleasing "clapter"—"message-driven comedy that inadvertently prioritizes political pandering above comedic merit"—instead of actual jokes. https://www.vulture.com/2018/01/the-rise-of-clapter-comedy.html [accessed 6/4/19]

2. As at least one of the hosts now admits. https://www.cnn.com/2015/02/12/opinion/begala-stewart-blew-up-crossfire/ [accessed 6/4/19]

3. (J. E. Campbell 2016, 61–90)

4. (J. E. Campbell 2016, 173–95; Theriault 2008)

5. (Groenendyk 2018; Mason 2018)

6. (Kalmoe and Mason 2019)

7. Recent books on polarization include (J. E. Campbell 2016; Fiorina 2017; Rosenfeld 2017; Hopkins 2017; Mason 2018).

8. (Fiorina and Abrams 2010; Fiorina 2017)

9. For discussion of this literature, see (Sunstein 2002, 2009).

10. We borrow this example from (Sunstein 2002, 175–76).

11. (Luskin et al. unpublished)

12. (Sunstein 2002, 176)

13. Indeed, a recent survey of political scientists ranked him as the worst president ever, a mere year into his first term: https://www.nytimes.com/interactive/2018/02/19/opinion/how-does-trump-stack-up-against-the-best-and-worst-presidents.html [accessed 9/15/18].

14. Rush Limbaugh: https://www.facebook.com/RushLimbaughAndTheEIB Network/posts/10153549717677906 [accessed 9/15/18] .

15. A Rasmussen poll: http://www.rasmussenreports.com/public_content/politics/current_events/bush_administration/41_say_bush_worst_president_ever_50_disagree [accessed 9/15/18].

16. (Will 2002, 238)
17. http://thehill.com/blogs/floor-action/house/363240-pelosi-gop-tax-proposal-the-worst-bill-in-the-history-of-the-united [accessed 3/5/18]
18. http://thehill.com/blogs/floor-action/house/363240-pelosi-gop-tax-proposal-the-worst-bill-in-the-history-of-the-united [accessed 3/5/18]
19. (Le Bon 1897, 34–35)
20. For discussions of the negative effects of widespread political ignorance, see (J. Brennan 2016; Achen and Bartels 2016; Caplan 2007; Somin 2013; Pincione and Tesón 2011).
21. (Oliver and Wood 2014)
22. http://www.newsweek.com/trump-birther-obama-poll-republicans-kenya-744195 [accessed 9/15/18]
23. (Ahler and Sood 2018; Graham, Nosek, and Haidt 2012)
24. The preceding figures are from (Ahler and Sood 2018).
25. (Somin 2013, 192)
26. (Walter and Murphy 2018)
27. Cognitive scientist Philip Fernbach and colleagues argue that people have an unjustified level of confidence in their understanding of social and political policies, such as the imposition of unilateral sanctions on Iran or transitioning to a single-payer health care system. When researchers asked these very confident subjects to *explain* how one of their preferred policies would work, they found that people then reported being less confident in their understanding of the policy and they also moderated their attitudes about that policy. The researchers hypothesize that asking subjects for an explanation of how things work forces them to confront their ignorance and moderate both their confidence and the extremity of their position (Fernbach et al. 2013).
28. (Yamamoto and Kushin 2014, 441). This research studied the relationship between online media and political disaffection during the 2008 U.S. presidential election campaign. We should note that the authors define cynicism differently than we do, using "political cynicism" to mean "a mistrustful disposition towards, and an absence of confidence in, the political system" ([Yamamoto and Kushin 2014, 431], citing [Austin and Pinkleton 1995, 1999]). Yamamoto and Kushin define "apathy" as "indifference towards, lack of interest in, or lack of attention to politics" ([2014, 432], citing [Bennett 1986]).
29. Citing (Jamieson 1992), Claes H. de Vreese defines strategic news as "news that focuses on winning and losing, is driven by 'war and games' language, emphasizes 'performers, critics and audiences,' focuses on candidate style and perceptions and gives weight to opinion polls" (de Vreese 2005, 284). For a variety of reasons, Cappella and Jamieson's conclusions, which focused on American subjects, have been revised and challenged in later research. For discussion of these responses and for studies of Dutch and Danish subjects, see (de Vreese 2005). Crucially, de Vreese claims that when media consumers are more sophisticated, the effects of strategic media in causing cynicism are largely mitigated.

30. For a more nuanced discussion of what it means for news to be framed as a "strategy" or as a "game," see (Aalberg, Strömbäck, and de Vreese 2012). In "game" frames, "race-horse journalism" focuses on opinion polls, election outcomes, and winners and losers, and it uses the language of sports and war. In "strategy" frames, journalists focus on campaign strategies and tactics, motives and instrumental actions, and personality and style, and utilize metacoverage (coverage of the media itself) (2012, 167). "The [most] cited element of the strategic frame," they write, "involves the journalistic focus on a candidate or a party's motives for taking a particular policy stand. Stories containing this element directly imply that political actors are primarily interested in garnering votes, rather than pursuing solutions for important social problems" (2012, 168).

31. (Kruger and Gilovich 1999)

32. (Williams 2007, 601)

33. Of course, the fact that we more readily conclude that those in our "out-group" are grandstanding doesn't show that grandstanding is purely in the eye of the beholder. Whether someone is grandstanding is a matter of fact, whether we are able to discover that fact or not.

34. (Mill 2017, 47)

35. Frankfurt gives the following illustrative example: "Spit-and-polish and red tape do not genuinely contribute, it is presumed, to the 'real' purposes of military personnel or government officials, even though they are imposed by agencies or agents that purport to be conscientiously devoted to the pursuit of those purposes. Thus the 'unnecessary routine tasks or ceremonial' that constitute bull are disconnected from the legitimating motives of the activity upon which they intrude, just as the things people say in bull sessions are disconnected from their settled beliefs, and as bullshit is disconnected from a concern with the truth" (Frankfurt 1988, 126–27).

36. In Richard Russo's novel *Straight Man*, the protagonist English professor Hank Devereaux, Jr. opines, "The student newspaper contains a lot more humor, though most of it unintentional. Except for the front page (campus news) and the back page (sports), the campus rag contains little but letters to the editor, which I scan first for allusions to myself and next for unusual content, which in the current climate is any subject other than the unholy trinity of insensitivity, sexism and bigotry, which the self-righteous, though not always literate, letter writers want their readers to know they're against. As a group they seem to believe that high moral indignation offsets and indeed outweighs all deficiencies of punctuation, spelling, grammar, logic, and style. In support of this notion there's only the entire culture" (Russo 1997, 73–74).

37. http://www.washingtonpost.com/wp-dyn/content/article/2006/06/23/AR2006062301378.html [accessed 7/22/18]

38. http://www.washingtonpost.com/wp-dyn/content/article/2006/06/23/AR2006062301378.html [accessed 7/22/18]

NOTES

39. In his 1793 translation, Samuel Croxall interpreted the fable as making a socio-political point: "when we are alarmed with imaginary dangers in respect of the public, till the cry grows quite stale and threadbare, how can it be expected we should know when to guard ourselves against real ones?" (Aesop and Croxall 1843, 224).
40. (Frijda 2006, 178–91)
41. (Frijda 2006, 10–11; Epstein 1973; McSweeney and Swindell 1999). Habituation is the reason that exposure therapy works as a treatment for PTSD, anxiety, and other conditions (Marks 1973; Foa 2011; Rothbaum et al. 2000; Feeny, Hembree, and Zoellner 2003).
42. (Goethe 1884, 75)
43. (Rothschild and Keefer 2017)
44. (Collins 1993, 210)
45. (Kaufman 1999, 140; Simon 1987)
46. (Fehr and Gächter 2002; Fehr and Fischbacher 2004)
47. (Dickinson and Masclet 2015)
48. For more evidence that people treat punishment as interchangeable with other responses to wrongdoing for purposes of seeking satisfaction, see (J. J. Jordan et al. 2016). There is also experimental evidence showing that people punish rather indiscriminately to promote cooperation, as they will do so even to support norms from which no one benefits (Abbink et al. 2017).
49. (Baier 1965, 3)
50. http://www.pewinternet.org/2016/10/25/the-political-environment-on-social-media/ [accessed 7/23/18]
51. For some interesting thoughts on why moderates in particular check out, see (Loury 1994, 435–38).
52. (Preoţiuc-Pietro et al. 2017)
53. (Noelle-Neumann 1993, 37–57)
54. (Jang, Lee, and Park 2014)
55. The arguments of this paragraph draw from John Stuart Mill's classic defense of free expression in On Liberty (1989, 19–55).
56. (Mutz 2006, 29–33)
57. (Frimer, Skitka, and Motyl 2017)
58. https://www.politico.com/magazine/story/2017/12/06/the-weird-campaign-to-get-taylor-swift-to-denounce-donald-trump-215994 [accessed 3/18/18]
59. https://www.politico.com/magazine/story/2017/12/06/the-weird-campaign-to-get-taylor-swift-to-denounce-donald-trump-215994 [accessed 3/8/18]
60. (Kogelmann and Wallace 2018)
61. https://www.usatoday.com/story/tech/2018/06/20/rage-giving-fuels-record-fundraising-immigrant-children/718272002/ [accessed 7/19/18]

62. https://www.usatoday.com/story/tech/2018/06/20/rage-giving-fuels-record-fundraising-immigrant-children/718272002/ [accessed 7/19/18]

Chapter 5

1. For an excellent psychological account of online shaming, see (Crockett 2017).
2. https://twitter.com/nickwiger/status/623968683807801344 [accessed 8/6/18]
3. (Ronson 2015, 231–38)
4. (Norlock 2017)
5. (Sawaoka and Monin 2018)
6. (Wellman 2012, 380–84)
7. (Audi 2015)
8. (Isenberg 1964, 466)
9. (Alicke et al. 2001)
10. (Merritt et al. 2012)
11. https://www.nytimes.com/2018/02/03/opinion/sunday/this-is-why-uma-thurman-is-angry.html [accessed 2/3/18]
12. To be fair, Dawkins himself tends to get angry pretty quickly in his exchanges with the religious. See, e.g., https://www.theguardian.com/world/2006/jan/13/religion.comment [accessed 2/6/18]
13. https://web.archive.org/web/20110920212327/http://seattletimes.nwsource.com/html/nationworld/2003365311_jesuscamp08.html [accessed 2/7/18]
14. (Green et al. 2019)
15. (Hardin 1968, 1244)
16. (Schmidtz 1994)
17. (Grice 1989)
18. (Hart 1955; Tosi 2018)
19. (Boyd and Richerson 1992)

Chapter 6

1. (MacIntyre 2007, 181–203; Hursthouse and Pettigrove 2018)
2. Virtue also requires, among other things, doing the right thing in the right kind of situation (she performs generous acts when they are called for) and across a variety of situations (she will not just be generous at home). It also requires a history of doing the right thing for the right reason (she didn't just start acting generously today).
3. Proponents of the traditional view, which also goes by the name Aristotelian virtue ethics, typically hold that virtue requires "acting for the right reasons

and with the right emotions" (van Zyl 2018, 23), with these two elements being in harmony. Our discussion simplifies the view in referring simply to a virtuous agent's motivations. For discussion, see (van Zyl 2018, 20–24; Annas 2011, 9–10; Hursthouse 2006, 101–5).

4. (C. Miller 2017, 151)

5. (Burtt 1990, 24)

6. We owe the aphorism to (Schmidtz 2008, 187).

7. Defenders of virtue consequentialism include (Hume 1998; Moore 1993; Driver 2001).

8. This version of virtue consequentialism is Julia Driver's (2001), which is perhaps the most developed account. But matters here are complicated and virtue consequentialists themselves disagree about what the view says. On these matters, see (Bradley 2005).

9. Again, as Bradley (2005) shows, matters are much more complicated than this, but this simplification suits our purposes.

10. (*Treatise of Human Nature*, 2.2.2.9). For a helpful discussion of Hume on vanity, see (Schliesser 2003, 334–35).

11. (*Treatise of Human Nature*, 3.2.2.12)

12. Hume writes, "When a man is prepossessed with a high notion of his rank and character in the creation, he will naturally endeavour to act up to it, and will scorn to do a base or vicious action, which might sink him below that figure which he makes in his own imagination" (Hume 2006, 317).

13. We thank Eric Schliesser for raising this question.

14. Adam Smith, for instance, thinks we should approve of vanity only when a person is vain about something worthy of vanity (A. Smith 1985, 255). Hume also seems to restrict his praise of vanity to those who are vain about virtuous action (Hume 2006, 321).

15. In our own studies, we found that grandstanding is not correlated with increased levels of civic engagement. See (Grubbs et al. 2019).

16. For an excellent survey of Nietzsche on morality, see (Leiter 2015).

17. (Nietzsche 1989, 107)

18. (Hurka 2007)

19. As Nietzsche saw things, the rise of Christianity accomplished just that. Those oppressed early Christians took their lowly, powerless qualities and turned them into moral virtues, such as modesty, humility, poverty, meekness, and patience. The oppressors might be noble and powerful, but they now become, after the revolt, morally evil. This is because they lack modesty, humility, poverty, meekness, and patience—the very qualities the early Christians just happened to have. After the revaluation of values, however, the meek, mild and powerless become virtuous. "Morality" as we have understood it since the rise of Christianity has, according to Nietzsche, frustrated the efforts of the most excellent, those who try to lead lives of genius and creativity. Christianity (as well as much other religious and moral thought) has turned true excellence on its head and made us feel

guilty for even wanting it. (Examples of the type of excellent people Nietzsche had in mind are Goethe, Beethoven, and Nietzsche himself.)

20. Eric Campbell has argued that inauthenticity plagues moral discourse, and that we are generally self-deceived about what motivates our moral expressions (E. Campbell 2014).

21. (Hurka 2010)

Chapter 7

1. https://www.thetimes.co.uk/article/politicians-must-stop-the-grandstanding-and-start-addressing-the-realities-dnr0w93fx [accessed 8/12/18]

2. https://www.washingtonpost.com/news/the-watch/wp/2018/05/11/the-protect-and-serve-act-is-political-grandstanding-over-a-nonexistent-problem-and-it-could-cause-real-harm/ [accessed 8/12/18]

3. https://www.bbc.com/news/av/world-us-canada-24308586/obama-attacks-republican-grandstanding [accessed 8/12/18]

4. https://www.nationalreview.com/bench-memos/president-obamas-grandstanding-signing-statements-ed-whelan/ [accessed 8/12/18]

5. (Hatemi and Fazekas 2018, 884)

6. For an interesting discussion of how activism conflicts with the pursuit of truth, see (van der Vossen 2015).

7. Political scientists have shown repeatedly that character is central in the mass public's assessment of politicians. See (A. H. Miller, Wattenberg, and Malanchuk 1986; Greene 2001; Hayes 2005; Bittner 2011; Clifford 2018).

8. http://archive.boston.com/news/nation/articles/2007/03/11/poll_character_trumps_policy_for_voters/ [accessed 8/12/18]

9. https://news.gallup.com/poll/12544/values-seen-most-important-characteristic-presidential-candidates.aspx [accessed 8/12/18]

10. http://archive.boston.com/news/nation/articles/2007/03/11/poll_character_trumps_policy_for_voters/ [accessed 8/12/18]

11. (Kahn and Kenney 1999; Druckman, Jacobs, and Ostermeier 2004)

12. (Kinder 1986)

13. (Bishin, Stevens, and Wilson 2005)

14. For a criticism of voting on the basis of character or a politician's values, see (J. Brennan 2011, 84–85). For a defense, see (Davis 2011).

15. Many recent books argue that most voters are ill-informed about politics, and that democracies therefore often fail to produce competent, responsible government (Caplan 2007; Somin 2013; J. Brennan 2016; Achen and Bartels 2016).

16. https://www.nytimes.com/2018/01/20/opinion/sunday/donald-trump-political-mythbuster.html [accessed 6/5/19]

17. For example, in Federalist No. 9, Alexander Hamilton voices the worry that instituting democracy on a large scale (even in a community the size of a U.S. state), would eventually result in "splitting ourselves into an infinity of little, jealous, clashing, tumultuous commonwealths, the wretched nurseries of unceasing discord, and the miserable objects of universal pity or contempt" (Hamilton, Madison, and Jay 2003, 37). Hamilton thought this would not be America's fate because of its decentralized design. See also James Madison's discussion of factions in Federalist No. 10 (Hamilton, Madison, and Jay 2003, 40–46).

18. (Vallier 2018)

19. https://www.salon.com/2014/11/20/ted_cruz_trolls_america_why_his_ new_lecture_on_responsible_governance_real_chutzpah/ [accessed 2/ 26/18]

20. Ibid.

21. (T. J. Ryan 2017)

22. (Dahl 1967, 53)

23. (Kreps, Laurin, and Merritt 2017)

24. As psychologist Jillian Jordan and her coauthors suggest, we tend to hate hypocrites because we take their high-minded moral pronouncements to be evidence of good character, and their later behavior reveals that their moral talk was a false signal (J. Jordan et al. 2017).

25. See, for example: http://thehill.com/opinion/katie-pavlich/255971 katie-pavlich-yes-obama-does-want-to-take-your-guns [accessed 8/13/18].

26. https://townhall.com/columnists/kurtschlichter/2017/02/06/the-left-hates-you-act-accordingly-n2281602 [accessed 7/18/18]

27. https://www.nytimes.com/2017/06/30/us/handmaids-protests-abortion. html [accessed 4/18/18]

28. https://www.newyorker.com/books/page-turner/we-live-in-the-reproductive-dystopia-of-the-handmaids-tale [accessed 4/18/18]

29. Shanto Iyengar and Masha Krupenkin show that, for Americans, hostility for the opposing party is now a greater motivation for political action than is positive identification with a party (2018).

30. http://www.nybooks.com/daily/2009/12/17/obama-and-the-rotten-compromise/ [accessed 9/24/18]

31. (Margalit 2009)

32. Fabian Wendt considers the following scenario: "imagine that a corrupt and brutal dictator wants financial support and international recognition, and offers his help in stabilizing the region and protecting some minority. Not achieving a compromise bears great risks: The dictator might feel free to behave in unpredictable ways that in the end might lead to instability and even war. Compared to all alternatives, it seems best to try to get a deal with the dictator" (Wendt 2019, 2871).

NOTES

33. This is the "median voter theorem" (Downs 1957), which says, roughly, that "a majority rule voting system will select the outcome most preferred by the median voter" (Holcombe 2006, 155). The extent of the theorem's applicability is still a matter of debate.

34. Political scientists James Adams and Samuel Merrill argue that "vote-seeking candidates are rewarded for presenting divergent policies that reflect the beliefs of voters biased toward them for non-policy reasons." This happens because politicians know that many voters will abstain if they find neither candidate sufficiently attractive and so they play to their bases on "considerations such as race, class, and partisanship, which are not entirely tied to the candidates' positions in the current campaign" (2003, 182).

35. See (Loury 1994, 441).

36. (Pincione and Tesón 2011, 124)

37. (Pincione and Tesón 2011, 124)

38. (G. Brennan and Lomasky 1997, 16)

39. For recent contributions to this literature, see (Caplan 2007; Somin 2013).

40. If reading this paragraph makes you anxious about the knowledge levels of your fellow citizens, you might be interested in a book on the case for epistocratic reforms. See (J. Brennan 2016).

41. (Pincione and Tesón 2011, 23) (emphasis in original).

42. (Nisbett and Ross 1980, 45). See also (Tuan Pham, Meyvis, and Zhou 2001).

43. See (Sloman and Fernbach 2017, 185).

44. Economist Paul Krugman, himself no supporter of unbridled free-markets, explains: "The analysis of rent control is among the best-understood issues in all of economics, and—among economists, anyway—one of the least controversial. In 1992, a poll of the American Economic Association found 93 percent of its members agreeing that 'a ceiling on rents reduces the quality and quantity of housing.' Almost every freshman-level textbook contains a case study on rent control, using its known adverse side effects to illustrate the principles of supply and demand. Sky-high rents on uncontrolled apartments, because desperate renters have nowhere to go—and the absence of new apartment construction, despite those high rents, because landlords fear that controls will be extended? Predictable. Bitter relations between tenants and landlords, with an arms race between ever-more ingenious strategies to force tenants out . . . constantly proliferating regulations designed to block those strategies? Predictable." https://www.nytimes.com/2000/06/07/opinion/reckonings-a-rent-affair.html [accessed 5/5/19]

45. In 2015, San Francisco Supervisor David Campos proposed halting development of market rate housing in the Mission neighborhood to deal with the city's housing crisis. Campos provided this vivid rationale: "The future of this neighborhood is riding on it. If we don't do this, we will lose the Mission. And if we lose the Mission, we will lose San Francisco. That's why we have to

act. And we have to act now." https://archives.sfexaminer.com/sanfrancisco/campos-to-propose-moratorium-on-market-rate-housing-in-the-mission/Content?oid=2928953 [accessed 7/11/18]

46. The reasons included severe fetal anomalies, rape, and saving the mother's life. The party disputed the budget figure, but apparently had no basis for an alternative estimate of the amount that it tried to decline. https://takingnote.blogs.nytimes.com/2012/06/20/anti-abortion-grandstanding/ [accessed 4/21/18]

47. (Vlahov and Junge 1998; Wodak and Cooney 2004)

48. (Pincione and Tesón 2011, 151)

49. (Pincione and Tesón 2011, 151)

50. (Ferguson 2012, 162) (emphasis added)

51. Guido Pincione coined the phrase "the paradox of solving social problems" in conversation.

52. "Barrett Wilson" is a pseudonym. https://quillette.com/2018/07/14/i-was-the-mob-until-the-mob-came-for-me/ [accessed 9/15/18]

53. (Bashir et al. 2013, 625)

54. (Christiano 2008, 61–63)

Chapter 8

1. See (Bond Jr and DePaulo 2006) for a meta-analysis of research on lying covering 24,000 total participants. As Von Hippel and Trivers (2011) argue, however, rates of detection are likely go up in situations where the deceived has a chance to cross-examine the deceiver and when they know each other.

2. (Vrij 2008). Evidence suggests that, on average, people lie once a day (DePaulo et al. 1996).

3. (Grubbs et al. 2019)

4. https://medium.com/@EamonCaddigan/accusations-of-virtue-signaling-are-fallacious-and-hypocritical-d86e9916e634 [accessed 9/27/18]

5. https://www.theguardian.com/commentisfree/2016/jan/20/virtue-signalling-putdown-passed-sell-by-date [accessed 9/27/18]

6. https://www.nytimes.com/2017/08/08/magazine/virtue-signaling-isnt-the-problem-not-believing-one-another-is.html [accessed 9/27/18]

7. https://www.newstatesman.com/politics/uk/2017/02/people-who-accuse-others-virtue-signalling-are-trying-stigmatise-empathy [accessed 9/27/18]

8. Psychologist Nick Haslam calls this "concept creep" (2016). He argues that concepts like abuse, bullying, trauma, addiction, and prejudice have had their meanings inflated among psychologists. See also (Levari et al. 2018).

9. Rebecca Solnit seems to have inspired the term after drawing attention to the phenomenon, though she did not coin it (Solnit 2015, 13–14).

10. https://www.nbcnews.com/news/world/prime-minister-theresa-may-accuses-labour-leader-jeremy-corbyn-mansplaining-n854641 [accessed 9/27/18]
11. (Wilde 1903, 11)
12. (Latané and Rodin 1969). See also (Latané and Darley 1970).
13. (Cann and Blackwelder 1984, 224)
14. (L. Ross and Nisbett 1991). Matthew Lieberman writes, "If a social psychologist was going to be marooned on a deserted island and could only take one principle of social psychology with him it would undoubtedly be 'the power of the situation'" (2005, 746).
15. (Gollwitzer and Oettingen 1998; Luszczynska, Sobczyk, and Abraham 2007; Chapman, Armitage, and Norman 2009)
16. (Gollwitzer et al. 2009)
17. (Gollwitzer et al. 2009)
18. For an outstanding analysis of the problem of open defecation in India, see (Coffey and Spears 2017).
19. (Bicchieri 2016)
20. The problem in India is due mostly to the latter issue. Indians are aware of the germ theory of disease. But they harbor mistaken beliefs about how often latrines must be emptied, and how much a suitable latrine costs. See (Coffey and Spears 2017, 67–73).
21. (Aikin and Talisse 2013). This discussion draws from https://news.vanderbilt.edu/vanderbiltmagazine/how-to-argue-advice-from-robert-talisse-and-scott-aikin/ [accessed 8/23/18].
22. Psychologists call this the "fundamental attribution error" (L. Ross and Nisbett 1991).
23. (Fullinwider 2005, 110). See also (Radzik 2012).
24. (Bicchieri 2016, 124). See also (Pascale, Sternin, and Sternin 2010).
25. (Elias 2000, 122)
26. (Elias 2000, 73)
27. (Elias 2000, 73)
28. (Elias 2000, 67)

BIBLIOGRAPHY

Aalberg, Toril, Jesper Strömbäck, and Claes H. de Vreese. 2012. "The Framing of Politics as Strategy and Game: A Review of Concepts, Operationalizations and Key Findings." *Journalism* 13 (2): 162–78. https://doi.org/10.1177/1464884911427799.

Abbink, Klaus, Lata Gangadharan, Toby Handfield, and John Thrasher. 2017. "Peer Punishment Promotes Enforcement of Bad Social Norms." *Nature Communications* 8 (1): 609. https://doi.org/10.1038/s41467-017-00731-0.

Achen, Christopher, and Larry Bartels. 2016. *Democracy for Realists: Why Elections Do Not Produce Responsive Government.* Princeton, NJ: Princeton University Press.

Adams, James, and Samuel Merrill. 2003. "Voter Turnout and Candidate Strategies in American Elections." *The Journal of Politics* 65 (1): 161–89. https://doi.org/10.1111/1468-2508.t01-1-00008.

Adelson, Rachel. 2004. "Detecting Deception." *APA Monitor on Psychology* 35 (7): 70–71.

Aesop, and Samuel Croxall. 1843. *The Fables of Aesop, with Instructive Applications.* Halifax: William Milner.

Ahler, Douglas J., and Gaurav Sood. 2018. "The Parties in Our Heads: Misperceptions about Party Composition and Their Consequences." *The Journal of Politics* 80 (3): 964–81. https://doi.org/10.1086/697253.

Aikin, Scott F., and Robert B. Talisse. 2013. *Why We Argue (And How We Should): A Guide to Political Disagreement.* New York: Routledge.

Alicke, Mark D., Debbie S. Vredenburg, Matthew Hiatt, and Olesya Govorun. 2001. "The 'Better Than Myself Effect.'" *Motivation and Emotion* 25 (1): 7–22. https://doi.org/10.1023/A:1010655705069.

Allison, Scott T., David M. Messick, and George R. Goethals. 1989. "On Being Better but Not Smarter Than Others: The Muhammad Ali Effect." *Social Cognition* 7 (3): 275–95. https://doi.org/10.1521/soco.1989.7.3.275.

Andersen, Hans Christian. 1993. *Andersen's Fairy Tales*. Ware, Hertfordshire: Wordsworth Editions.

Annas, Julia. 2011. *Intelligent Virtue*. Oxford: Oxford University Press.

Asch, Solomon E. 1956. "Studies of Independence and Conformity: A Minority of One Against a Unanimous Majority." *Psychological Monographs: General and Applied* 70 (9): 1–70.

Audi, Robert. 2015. *Means, Ends, and Persons: The Meaning and Psychological Dimensions of Kant's Humanity Formula*. Oxford: Oxford University Press.

Austin, Erica Weintraub, and Bruce E. Pinkleton. 1995. "Positive and Negative Effects of Political Disaffection on the Less Experienced Voter." *Journal of Broadcasting & Electronic Media* 39 (2): 215–35. https://doi.org/10.1080/08838159509364300.

Austin, Erica Weintraub, and Bruce E. Pinkleton. 1999. "The Relation Between Media Content Evaluations and Political Disaffection." *Mass Communication and Society* 2 (3–4): 105–22. https://doi.org/10.1080/15205436.1999.9677867.

Baier, Kurt. 1965. *The Moral Point of View: A Rational Basis of Ethics*. Abridged. New York: Random House.

Bashir, Nadia Y., Penelope Lockwood, Alison L. Chasteen, Daniel Nadolny, and Indra Noyes. 2013. "The Ironic Impact of Activists: Negative Stereotypes Reduce Social Change Influence." *European Journal of Social Psychology* 43 (7): 614–26. https://doi.org/10.1002/ejsp.1983.

Bennett, Stephen Earl. 1986. *Apathy in America, 1960-1984: Causes and Consequences of Citizen Political Indifference*. Dobbs Ferry, NY: Transnational Publishers.

Berry, Jeffrey M., and Sarah Sobieraj. 2014. *The Outrage Industry: Political Opinion Media and the New Incivility*. Oxford: Oxford University Press.

Bicchieri, Cristina. 2016. *Norms in the Wild: How to Diagnose, Measure, and Change Social Norms*. New York: Oxford University Press.

Bishin, Benjamin G., Daniel Stevens, and Christian Wilson. 2005. "Truth or Consequences?: Character and Swing Voters in the 2000 Election." *Public Integrity* 7 (2): 129–46. https://doi.org/10.1080/10999922.2005.11051273.

Bittner, Amanda. 2011. *Platform or Personality?: The Role of Party Leaders in Elections*. New York: Oxford University Press.

Bond Jr, Charles F., and Bella M. DePaulo. 2006. "Accuracy of Deception Judgments." *Personality and Social Psychology Review* 10 (3): 214–34.

Bond, Rod, and Peter B. Smith. 1996. "Culture and Conformity: A Meta-Analysis of Studies Using Asch's Line Judgment Task." *Psychological Bulletin* 119 (1): 111–37. https://doi.org/10.1037/0033-2909.119.1.111.

Boyd, Robert, and Peter J. Richerson. 1992. "Punishment Allows the Evolution of Cooperation (or Anything Else) in Sizable Groups." *Ethology and Sociobiology* 13 (3): 171–95. https://doi.org/10.1016/0162-3095(92)90032-Y.

Bradley, Ben. 2005. "Virtue Consequentialism." *Utilitas* 17 (3): 282–98. https://doi.org/10.1017/S0953820805001652.

Brennan, Geoffrey, and Loren Lomasky. 1997. *Democracy and Decision: The Pure Theory of Electoral Preference*. Cambridge, UK: Cambridge University Press.

Brennan, Jason. 2011. *The Ethics of Voting*. Princeton, NJ: Princeton University Press.

Brennan, Jason. 2016. *Against Democracy*. Princeton, NJ: Princeton University Press. https://press.princeton.edu/titles/10843.html.

Brown, Jonathon D. 2012. "Understanding the Better Than Average Effect: Motives (Still) Matter." *Personality and Social Psychology Bulletin* 38 (2): 209–19. https://doi.org/10.1177/0146167211432763.

Burtt, Shelley. 1990. "The Good Citizen's Psyche: On the Psychology of Civic Virtue." *Polity* 23 (1): 23–38. https://doi.org/10.2307/3235141.

Buss, David M., and Lisa A. Dedden. 1990. "Derogation of Competitors." *Journal of Social and Personal Relationships* 7 (3): 395–422.

Campbell, Eric. 2014. "Breakdown of Moral Judgment." *Ethics* 124 (3): 447–80. https://doi.org/10.1086/674845.

Campbell, James E. 2016. *Polarized: Making Sense of a Divided America*. Princeton, NJ: Princeton University Press. https://press.princeton.edu/titles/10846.html.

Cann, Arnie, and Jill Goodman Blackwelder. 1984. "Compliance and Mood: A Field Investigation of the Impact of Embarrassment." *The Journal of Psychology* 117 (2): 221–26. https://doi.org/10.1080/00223980.1984.9923681.

Caplan, Bryan. 2007. *The Myth of the Rational Voter: Why Democracies Choose Bad Policies*. Princeton, NJ: Princeton University Press.

Caplan, Bryan. 2018. *The Case Against Education: Why the Education System Is a Waste of Time and Money*. Princeton, NJ: Princeton University Press.

Cappella, Joseph N., and Kathleen Hall Jamieson. 1997. *Spiral of Cynicism: The Press and the Public Good*. New York: Oxford University Press.

Chapman, Janine, Christopher J. Armitage, and Paul Norman. 2009. "Comparing Implementation Intention Interventions in Relation to Young Adults' Intake of Fruit and Vegetables." *Psychology and Health* 24 (3): 317–32.

Cheng, Joey T., Jessica L. Tracy, and Joseph Henrich. 2010. "Pride, Personality, and the Evolutionary Foundations of Human Social Status." *Evolution and Human Behavior* 31 (5): 334–47. https://doi.org/10.1016/j.evolhumbehav.2010.02.004.

Christiano, Thomas. 2008. *The Constitution of Equality: Democratic Authority and Its Limits*. Oxford: Oxford University Press.

Clifford, Scott. 2018. "Reassessing the Structure of Presidential Character." *Electoral Studies* 54 (August): 240–47. https://doi.org/10.1016/j.electstud.2018.04.006.

Coffey, Diane, and Dean Spears. 2017. *Where India Goes: Abandoned Toilets, Stunted Development and the Costs of Caste*. Noida, Uttar Pradesh: HarperCollins India.

Collins, Randall. 1993. "Emotional Energy as the Common Denominator of Rational Action." *Rationality and Society* 5 (2): 203–30. https://doi.org/10.1177/1043463193005002005.

Crockett, M. J. 2017. "Moral Outrage in the Digital Age." *Nature Human Behaviour* 1 (11): 769. https://doi.org/10.1038/s41562-017-0213-3.

Cross, K. Patricia. 1977. "Not Can, but Will College Teaching Be Improved?" *New Directions for Higher Education* 17: 1–15. https://doi.org/10.1002/he.36919771703.

Dahl, Robert Alan. 1967. *Pluralist Democracy in the United States: Conflict and Consent.* Chicago: Rand McNally.

Davis, Ryan W. 2011. "A Moral Defense of the 'Moral Values' Voter." *Political Studies* 59 (4): 996–1016. https://doi.org/10.1111/j.1467-9248.2011.00888.x.

DePaulo, Bella M., Deborah A. Kashy, Susan E. Kirkendol, Melissa M. Wyer, and Jennifer A. Epstein. 1996. "Lying in Everyday Life." *Journal of Personality and Social Psychology* 70 (5): 979–95. https://doi.org/10.1037/0022-3514.70.5.979.

Dickinson, David L., and David Masclet. 2015. "Emotion Venting and Punishment in Public Good Experiments." *Journal of Public Economics* 122 (February): 55–67. https://doi.org/10.1016/j.jpubeco.2014.10.008.

Downs, Anthony. 1957. *An Economic Theory of Democracy.* New York: Harper.

Driver, Julia. 2001. *Uneasy Virtue.* Cambridge, UK: Cambridge University Press.

Driver, Julia. 2005. "Moralism." *Journal of Applied Philosophy* 22 (2): 137–51. https://doi.org/10.1111/j.1468-5930.2005.00298.x.

Druckman, James N., Lawrence R. Jacobs, and Eric Ostermeier. 2004. "Candidate Strategies to Prime Issues and Image." *The Journal of Politics* 66 (4): 1180–1202.

Dunning, David. 2016. "False Moral Superiority." In *The Social Psychology of Good and Evil,* edited by Arthur G. Miller, 2nd ed., 171–84. New York: The Guilford Press.

Elias, Norbert. 2000. *The Civilizing Process: Sociogenetic and Psychogenetic Investigations.* 2nd ed. Malden, MA: Wiley.

Epley, Nicholas, and David Dunning. 2000. "Feeling 'Holier Than Thou': Are Self-Serving Assessments Produced by Errors in Self- or Social Prediction?" *Journal of Personality and Social Psychology* 79 (6): 861–75.

Epstein, Seymour. 1973. "Expectancy and Magnitude of Reaction to a Noxious UCS." *Psychophysiology* 10 (1): 100–107. https://doi.org/10.1111/j.1469-8986.1973.tb01091.x.

Feeny, Norah C., Elizabeth A. Hembree, and Lori A. Zoellner. 2003. "Myths Regarding Exposure Therapy for PTSD." *Cognitive and Behavioral Practice* 10 (1): 85–90. https://doi.org/10.1016/S1077-7229(03)80011-1.

Fehr, Ernst, and Urs Fischbacher. 2004. "Third-Party Punishment and Social Norms." *Evolution and Human Behavior* 25 (2): 63–87. https://doi.org/10.1016/S1090-5138(04)00005-4.

Fehr, Ernst, and Simon Gächter. 2002. "Altruistic Punishment in Humans." *Nature* 415 (January): 137–40.

Ferguson, Michaele L. 2012. *Sharing Democracy.* New York: Oxford University Press.

Fernbach, Philip M., Todd Rogers, Craig R. Fox, and Steven A. Sloman. 2013. "Political Extremism Is Supported by an Illusion of Understanding." *Psychological Science* 24 (6): 939–46. https://doi.org/10.1177/0956797612464058.

Festinger, Leon. 1954. "A Theory of Social Comparison Processes." *Human Relations* 7 (2): 117–40.

Fetchenhauer, Detlev, and David Dunning. 2006. "Perception of Prosociality in Self and Others." In *Solidarity and Prosocial Behavior: An Integration of Psychological and Sociological Perspectives*, edited by Detlev Fetchenhauer, Andreas Flache, Abraham P. Buunk, and Siegwart M. Lindenberg, 61–76. New York: Kluwer Academic/ Plenum Publishers. https://www.rug.nl/research/portal/en/publications/ perception-of-prosociality-in-self-and-others(5e1deb73-d787-41b7-8b61- 65472d68a940).html.

Fields, James M., and Howard Schuman. 1976. "Public Beliefs About the Beliefs of the Public." *Public Opinion Quarterly* 40 (4): 427–48. https://doi.org/10.1086/ 268330.

Fiorina, Morris P. 2017. *Unstable Majorities: Polarization, Party Sorting, and Political Stalemate*. Stanford, CA: Hoover Institution Press.

Fiorina, Morris P., and Samuel Abrams. 2010. "Where's the Polarization?" In *Controversies in Voting Behavior*, edited by Richard G. Niemi, Herbert F. Weisberg, and David C. Kimball, 5th ed., 309–18. Washington, DC: CQ Press.

Foa, Edna B. 2011. "Prolonged Exposure Therapy: Past, Present, and Future." *Depression and Anxiety* 28 (12): 1043–47. https://doi.org/10.1002/ da.20907.

Frankfurt, Harry G. 1988. "On Bullshit." In *The Importance of What We Care About: Philosophical Essays*, 117–33. Cambridge, UK: Cambridge University Press.

Frijda, Nico H. 2006. *The Laws of Emotion*. Mahwah, NJ: Psychology Press.

Frimer, Jeremy A., Linda J. Skitka, and Matt Motyl. 2017. "Liberals and Conservatives Are Similarly Motivated to Avoid Exposure to One Another's Opinions." *Journal of Experimental Social Psychology* 72: 1–12. https://doi.org/10.1016/ j.jesp.2017.04.003.

Fullinwider, Robert K. 2005. "On Moralism." *Journal of Applied Philosophy* 22 (2): 105–20.

Goethals, George R. 1986. "Social Comparison Theory: Psychology from the Lost and Found." *Personality and Social Psychology Bulletin* 12 (3): 261–78. https:// doi.org/10.1177/0146167286123001.

Goethals, George R., David M. Messick, and Scott T. Allison. 1991. "The Uniqueness Bias: Studies of Constructive Social Comparison." In *Social Comparison: Contemporary Theory and Research*, edited by Jerry Suls and Thomas Ashby Wills, 149–76. Hillsdale, NJ: Erlbaum.

Goethe, Johann Wolfgang von. 1884. *The Sorrows of Werther: Elective Affinities and a Nouvelette*. Translated by R. Dillon Boylan. Boston: S. E. Cassino.

Goffman, Erving. 1959. *The Presentation of Self in Everyday Life*. New York: Anchor.

Gollwitzer, Peter M., and Gabriele Oettingen. 1998. "The Emergence and Implementation of Health Goals." *Psychology and Health* 13 (4): 687–715.

Gollwitzer, Peter M., Frank Wieber, Andrea L. Myers, and Sean M. McCrea. 2009. "How to Maximize Implementation Intention Effects." In *Then A Miracle Occurs: Focusing on Behavior in Social Psychological Theory and Research*, edited by Christopher R. Agnew, Donal E. Carlston, William G. Graziano, and Janice R. Kelly, 137–61. Oxford: Oxford University Press. http://www.oxfordscholarship.com/view/10.1093/acprof:oso/9780195377798.001.0001/acprof-9780195377798-chapter-8.

Graham, Jesse, Brian A. Nosek, and Jonathan Haidt. 2012. "The Moral Stereotypes of Liberals and Conservatives: Exaggeration of Differences across the Political Spectrum." *PLOS ONE* 7 (12): e50092. https://doi.org/10.1371/journal.pone.0050092.

Green, Jeffrey D., Constantine Sedikides, Daryl R. Van Tongeren, Anna M. C. Behler, and Jessica M. Barber. 2019. "Self-Enhancement, Righteous Anger, and Moral Grandiosity." *Self and Identity* 18 (2): 201–16. https://doi.org/10.1080/15298868.2017.1419504.

Greene, Steven. 2001. "The Role of Character Assessments in Presidential Approval." *American Politics Research* 29 (2): 196–210.

Grice, H. Paul. 1989. "Logic and Conversation." In *Studies in the Way of Words*, 22–40. Cambridge, MA: Harvard University Press.

Groenendyk, Eric. 2018. "Competing Motives in a Polarized Electorate: Political Responsiveness, Identity Defensiveness, and the Rise of Partisan Antipathy." *Political Psychology* 39: 159–71. https://doi.org/10.1111/pops.12481.

Grubbs, Joshua B., Brandon Warmke, Justin Tosi, A. Shanti James, and W. Keith Campbell. 2019. "Moral Grandstanding in Public Discourse: Status-Seeking Motives as a Potential Explanatory Mechanism in Predicting Conflict." Preprint. PsyArXiv. https://doi.org/10.31234/osf.io/gnaj5.

Haidt, Jonathan. 2012. *The Righteous Mind: Why Good People Are Divided by Politics and Religion*. New York: Vintage.

Hamilton, Alexander, James Madison, and John Jay. 2003. *The Federalist: With Letters of Brutus*. Edited by Terence Ball. Cambridge, UK: Cambridge University Press.

Hardin, Garrett. 1968. "The Tragedy of the Commons." *Science* 162 (3859): 1243–48. https://doi.org/10.1126/science.162.3859.1243.

Hart, H. L. A. 1955. "Are There Any Natural Rights?" *Philosophical Review* 64: 175–91.

Haslam, Nick. 2016. "Concept Creep: Psychology's Expanding Concepts of Harm and Pathology." *Psychological Inquiry* 27 (1): 1–17. https://doi.org/10.1080/1047840X.2016.1082418.

Hatemi, Peter K., and Zoltán Fazekas. 2018. "Narcissism and Political Orientations." *American Journal of Political Science* 62 (4): 873–88. https://doi.org/10.1111/ajps.12380.

Hayes, Danny. 2005. "Candidate Qualities through a Partisan Lens: A Theory of Trait Ownership." *American Journal of Political Science* 49 (4): 908–23.

Heck, Patrick R., and Joachim I. Krueger. 2016. "Social Perception of Self-Enhancement Bias and Error." *Social Psychology* 47 (6): 327–39. https://doi.org/10.1027/1864-9335/a000287.

Henrich, Joseph. 2015. *The Secret of Our Success*. Princeton, NJ: Princeton University Press. https://press.princeton.edu/titles/10543.html.

Hippel, William von, and Robert Trivers. 2011. "The Evolution and Psychology of Self-Deception." *Behavioral and Brain Sciences* 34 (1): 1–16. https://doi.org/10.1017/S0140525X10001354.

Holcombe, Randall G. 2006. *Public Sector Economics: The Role of Government in the American Economy*. Upper Saddle River, NJ: Pearson.

Honts, Charles R., and John C. Kircher. 1994. "Mental and Physical Countermeasures Reduce the Accuracy of Polygraph Tests." *Journal of Applied Psychology* 79 (2): 252–59. https://doi.org/10.1037/0021-9010.79.2.252.

Hopkins, David A. 2017. *Red Fighting Blue: How Geography and Electoral Rules Polarize American Politics*. Cambridge, UK: Cambridge University Press.

Hume, David. 1998. *An Enquiry Concerning the Principles of Morals*. New York: Oxford University Press.

Hume, David. 2006. *Moral Philosophy*. Edited by Geoffrey Sayre-McCord. Indianapolis: Hackett.

Hurka, Thomas. 2007. "Nietzsche: Perfectionist." In *Nietzsche and Morality*, edited by Brian Leiter and Neil Sinhababu, 9–31. New York: Oxford University Press.

Hurka, Thomas. 2010. *The Best Things in Life: A Guide to What Really Matters*. New York: Oxford University Press.

Hursthouse, Rosalind. 2006. "Are Virtues the Proper Starting Point for Morality?" In *Contemporary Debates in Moral Theory*, edited by James Dreier, 99–112. Malden, MA: Blackwell.

Hursthouse, Rosalind, and Glen Pettigrove. 2018. "Virtue Ethics." In *The Stanford Encyclopedia of Philosophy*, edited by Edward N. Zalta, Winter 2018. Metaphysics Research Lab, Stanford University. https://plato.stanford.edu/archives/win2018/entries/ethics-virtue/.

Isenberg, Arnold. 1964. "Deontology and the Ethics of Lying." *Philosophy and Phenomenological Research* 24 (4): 463–480.

Iyengar, Shanto, and Masha Krupenkin. 2018. "The Strengthening of Partisan Affect." *Political Psychology* 39 (S1): 201–18. https://doi.org/10.1111/pops.12487.

Jamie, Gabriel A. 2017. "Signals, Cues and the Nature of Mimicry." *Proceedings of the Royal Society B: Biological Sciences* 284 (1849). https://doi.org/10.1098/rspb.2016.2080.

Jamieson, Kathleen Hall. 1992. *Dirty Politics: Deception, Distraction, and Democracy*. New York: Oxford University Press.

Jang, S. Mo, Hoon Lee, and Yong Jin Park. 2014. "The More Friends, the Less Political Talk? Predictors of Facebook Discussions Among College Students." *Cyberpsychology, Behavior, and Social Networking* 17 (5): 271–75. https://doi.org/10.1089/cyber.2013.0477.

Jordan, Jillian J., Moshe Hoffman, Paul Bloom, and David G. Rand. 2016. "Third-Party Punishment as a Costly Signal of Trustworthiness." *Nature* 530 (7591): 473. https://doi.org/10.1038/nature16981.

Jordan, Jillian, Roseanna Sommers, Paul Bloom, and David Rand. 2017. "Why Do We Hate Hypocrites? Evidence for a Theory of False Signaling." SSRN Scholarly Paper ID 2897313. Rochester, NY: Social Science Research Network. https://papers.ssrn.com/abstract=2897313.

Kahn, Kim Fridkin, and Patrick J. Kenney. 1999. *The Spectacle of US Senate Campaigns.* Princeton, NJ: Princeton University Press.

Kalmoe, Nathan P., and Lilliana Mason. 2019. "Lethal Mass Partisanship: Prevalence, Correlates, & Electoral Contingencies." Paper presented at the 2018 American Political Science Association's Annual Meeting, Boston, Aug. 30–Sept. 2.

Kaufman, Bruce E. 1999. "Emotional Arousal as a Source of Bounded Rationality." *Journal of Economic Behavior & Organization* 38 (2): 135–44. https://doi.org/10.1016/S0167-2681(99)00002-5.

Kelly, Michael J. 1888. *Play Ball: Stories of the Ball Field.* Boston: Emery and Hughes.

Kennedy, Jessica, and Maurice E. Schweitzer. 2015. "Holding People Responsible for Ethical Violations: The Surprising Benefits of Accusing Others." *Academy of Management Proceedings* 2015 (1): 112–58. https://doi.org/10.5465/ambpp.2015.11258abstract.

Kinder, Donald. 1986. "Presidential Character Revisited." In *Political Cognition,* edited by Richard Lau and David Sears, 233–56. Hillsdale, NJ: Erlbaum.

Klein, Nadav, and Nicholas Epley. 2016. "Maybe Holier, but Definitely Less Evil, than You: Bounded Self-Righteousness in Social Judgment." *Journal of Personality and Social Psychology* 110 (5): 660.

Klein, Nadav, and Nicholas Epley. 2017. "Less Evil Than You: Bounded Self-Righteousness in Character Inferences, Emotional Reactions, and Behavioral Extremes." *Personality and Social Psychology Bulletin* 43 (8): 1202–12. https://doi.org/10.1177/0146167217711918.

Kogelmann, Brian, and Robert H. Wallace. 2018. "Moral Diversity and Moral Responsibility." *Journal of the American Philosophical Association* 4 (3): 371–89.

Kreps, Tamar A., Kristin Laurin, and Anna C. Merritt. 2017. "Hypocritical Flip-Flop, or Courageous Evolution? When Leaders Change Their Moral Minds." *Journal of Personality and Social Psychology* 113 (5): 730–52. https://doi.org/10.1037/pspi0000103.

Kruger, Justin, and Thomas Gilovich. 1999. "'Naive Cynicism' in Everyday Theories of Responsibility Assessment: On Biased Assumptions of Bias." *Journal of*

Personality and Social Psychology 76 (5): 743–53. https://doi.org/10.1037/ 0022-3514.76.5.743.

Kuran, Timur. 1995. *Private Truths, Public Lies: The Social Consequences of Preference Falsification.* Cambridge, MA: Harvard University Press.

Lange, Paul A. M. van, and Constantine Sedikides. 1998. "Being More Honest but Not Necessarily More Intelligent than Others: Generality and Explanations for the Muhammad Ali Effect." *European Journal of Social Psychology* 28 (4): 675–80. https://doi.org/10.1002/(SICI)1099-0992(199807/ 08)28:4<675::AID-EJSP883>3.0.CO;2-5.

Latané, Bibb, and John M. Darley. 1970. *The Unresponsive Bystander: Why Doesn't He Help?* New York: Appleton-Century Crofts.

Latané, Bibb, and Judith Rodin. 1969. "A Lady in Distress: Inhibiting Effects of Friends and Strangers on Bystander Intervention." *Journal of Experimental Social Psychology* 5 (2): 189–202. https://doi.org/10.1016/0022-1031(69)90046-8.

Laurent, Sean M., Brian A. M. Clark, Stephannie Walker, and Kimberly D. Wiseman. 2014. "Punishing Hypocrisy: The Roles of Hypocrisy and Moral Emotions in Deciding Culpability and Punishment of Criminal and Civil Moral Transgressors." *Cognition & Emotion* 28 (1): 59–83. https://doi.org/10.1080/ 02699931.2013.801339.

Leary, Mark R., and Robin M. Kowalski. 1990. "Impression Management: A Literature Review and Two-Component Model." *Psychological Bulletin* 107 (1): 34–47. https://doi.org/10.1037/0033-2909.107.1.34.

Leiter, Brian. 2015. *Nietzsche on Morality.* 2nd ed. London: Routledge.

Levari, David E., Daniel T. Gilbert, Timothy D. Wilson, Beau Sievers, David M. Amodio, and Thalia Wheatley. 2018. "Prevalence-Induced Concept Change in Human Judgment." *Science* 360 (6396): 1465–67. https://doi.org/10.1126/ science.aap8731.

Lieberman, Matthew D. 2005. "Principles, Processes, and Puzzles of Social Cognition: An Introduction for the Special Issue on Social Cognitive Neuroscience." *NeuroImage* 28 (4): 745–56. https://doi.org/10.1016/j.neuroimage.2005.07.028.

Liu, Ying. 2013. "Investigating the Relation between Moral Self-Enhancement and Self-Deception: A Cross-Cultural Study of U.S. and Chinese College Students." *Dissertations* 279 (December). https://irl.umsl.edu/dissertation/279.

Loury, Glenn C. 1994. "Self-Censorship in Public Discourse: A Theory of 'Political Correctness' and Related Phenomena." *Rationality and Society* 6 (4): 428–61.

Luskin, Robert C., Gaurav Sood, James S. Fishkin, and Kyu S. Hahn. unpublished. "Deliberative Distortions? Homogenization, Polarization, and Domination in Small Group Deliberations."

Luszczynska, Aleksandra, Anna Sobczyk, and Charles Abraham. 2007. "Planning to Lose Weight: Randomized Controlled Trial of an Implementation Intention Prompt to Enhance Weight Reduction among Overweight and Obese Women." *Health Psychology* 26 (4): 507–12.

MacIntyre, Alasdair. 2007. *After Virtue: A Study in Moral Theory, Third Edition.* 3rd ed. Notre Dame, IN: University of Notre Dame Press.

Margalit, Avishai. 2009. *On Compromise and Rotten Compromises.* Princeton, NJ: Princeton University Press.

Marks, Isaac M. 1973. "Reduction of Fear: Towards a Unifying Theory." *Canadian Psychiatric Association Journal* 18 (1): 9–12. https://doi.org/10.1177/070674377301800103.

Marques, José M., Vincent Y. Yzerbyt, and Jacques-Philippe Leyens. 1988. "The 'Black Sheep Effect': Extremity of Judgments towards Ingroup Members as a Function of Group Identification." *European Journal of Social Psychology* 18 (1): 1–16. https://doi.org/10.1002/ejsp.2420180102.

Mason, Lilliana. 2018. *Uncivil Agreement.* Chicago: Chicago University Press. https://www.press.uchicago.edu/ucp/books/book/chicago/U/bo27527354.html.

McGrath, Robert. 2015. "Character Strengths in 75 Nations: An Update." *The Journal of Positive Psychology* 10: 41–52. https://doi.org/10.1080/17439760.2014.888580.

McSweeney, Frances K., and Samantha Swindell. 1999. "General-Process Theories of Motivation Revisited: The Role of Habituation." *Psychological Bulletin* 125 (4): 437.

Merritt, Anna C., Daniel A. Effron, Steven Fein, Kenneth K. Savitsky, Daniel M. Tuller, and Benoît Monin. 2012. "The Strategic Pursuit of Moral Credentials." *Journal of Experimental Social Psychology* 48 (3): 774–77. https://doi.org/10.1016/j.jesp.2011.12.017.

Mill, John Stuart. 1989. *On Liberty and Other Writings.* Cambridge, UK: Cambridge University Press.

Mill, John Stuart. 2017. *Utilitarianism: With Related Remarks from Mill's Other Writings.* Indianapolis: Hackett.

Miller, Arthur H., Martin P. Wattenberg, and Oksana Malanchuk. 1986. "Schematic Assessments of Presidential Candidates." *American Political Science Review* 80 (2): 521–40.

Miller, Christian. 2017. *The Character Gap: How Good Are We?* Oxford: Oxford University Press.

Moliere, Jean-Baptiste Poquelin. 2008. *The Misanthrope.* Translated by Ranjit Bolt. London: Oberon Books. https://books.google.com/books?id=eTd4nzL7Sj0C.

Möller, Jens, and Karel Savyon. 2003. "Not Very Smart, Thus Moral: Dimensional Comparisons Between Academic Self-Concept and Honesty." *Social Psychology of Education* 6 (2): 95–106. https://doi.org/10.1023/A:1023247910033.

Moore, G. E. 1993. *Principia Ethica.* Cambridge, UK: Cambridge University Press.

Mullen, Elizabeth, and Linda J. Skitka. 2006. "When Outcomes Prompt Criticism of Procedures: An Analysis of the Rodney King Case." *Analyses of Social Issues and Public Policy* 6 (1): 1–14. https://doi.org/10.1111/j.1530-2415.2006.00100.x.

Mutz, Diana C. 2006. *Hearing the Other Side: Deliberative versus Participatory Democracy.* Cambridge, UK: Cambridge University Press.

Nietzsche, Friedrich. 1989. *On the Genealogy of Morals and Ecce Homo.* Edited by Walter Kaufmann. Reissue edition. New York: Vintage.

Nisbett, Richard E., and Lee Ross. 1980. *Human Inference: Strategies and Shortcomings of Social Judgment.* Englewood Cliffs, NJ: Prentice-Hall.

Nisbett, Richard E., and Timothy D. Wilson. 1977. "Telling More Than We Can Know: Verbal Reports on Mental Processes." *Psychological Review* 84 (3): 231–59. https://doi.org/10.1037/0033-295X.84.3.231.

Noelle-Neumann, Elisabeth. 1993. *The Spiral of Silence: Public Opinion—Our Social Skin.* 2nd ed. Chicago: University of Chicago Press.

Norlock, Kathryn J. 2017. "Online Shaming." *Social Philosophy Today* 33 (June): 187–97. https://doi.org/10.5840/socphiltoday201762343.

Norris, Robert S., and Hans M. Kristensen. 2006. "Global Nuclear Stockpiles, 1945–2006." *Bulletin of the Atomic Scientists* 62 (4): 64–66. https://doi.org/10.2968/062004017.

Nozick, Robert. 1990. *The Examined Life: Philosophical Meditations.* New York: Simon & Schuster.

Oliver, J. Eric, and Thomas J. Wood. 2014. "Conspiracy Theories and the Paranoid Style(s) of Mass Opinion." *American Journal of Political Science* 58 (4): 952–66.

Pascale, Richard, Jerry Sternin, and Monique Sternin. 2010. *The Power of Positive Deviance: How Unlikely Innovators Solve the World's Toughest Problems.* 1st ed. Boston: Harvard Business Review Press.

Pincione, Guido, and Fernando R. Tesón. 2011. *Rational Choice and Democratic Deliberation: A Theory of Discourse Failure.* New York: Cambridge University Press.

Pinker, Steven, Martin A. Nowak, and James J. Lee. 2008. "The Logic of Indirect Speech." *Proceedings of the National Academy of Sciences* 105 (3): 833–38. https://doi.org/10.1073/pnas.0707192105.

Pinto, Isabel R., José M. Marques, John M. Levine, and Dominic Abrams. 2010. "Membership Status and Subjective Group Dynamics: Who Triggers the Black Sheep Effect?" *Journal of Personality and Social Psychology* 99 (1): 107–19.

Powell, Caitlin A. J., and Richard H. Smith. 2013. "Schadenfreude Caused by the Exposure of Hypocrisy in Others." *Self and Identity* 12 (4): 413–31.

Preble, Christopher A. 2003. "'Who Ever Believed in the "Missile Gap"?': John F. Kennedy and the Politics of National Security." *Presidential Studies Quarterly* 33 (4): 801–26. https://doi.org/10.1046/j.0360-4918.2003.00085.x.

Preoţiuc-Pietro, Daniel, Ye Liu, Daniel Hopkins, and Lyle Ungar. 2017. "Beyond Binary Labels: Political Ideology Prediction of Twitter Users." In *Proceedings of the 55th Annual Meeting of the Association for Computational Linguistics,* 729–40. Vancouver: Association for Computational Linguistics. https://doi.org/10.18653/v1/P17-1068.

Radzik, Linda. 2012. "On the Virtue of Minding Our Own Business." *The Journal of Value Inquiry* 46 (2): 173–82. https://doi.org/10.1007/s10790-012-9317-1.

Rom, Sarah C., and Paul Conway. 2018. "The Strategic Moral Self: Self-Presentation Shapes Moral Dilemma Judgments." *Journal of Experimental Social Psychology* 74 (January): 24–37. https://doi.org/10.1016/j.jesp.2017.08.003.

Ronson, Jon. 2015. *So You've Been Publicly Shamed.* New York: Riverhead Books.

Rosenfeld, Sam. 2017. *The Polarizers: Postwar Architects of Our Partisan Era.* Chicago: University of Chicago Press.

Ross, Lee, and Richard E Nisbett. 1991. *The Person and the Situation: Perspectives of Social Psychology.* New York: McGraw-Hill.

Ross, Michael, and Fiore Sicoly. 1979. "Egocentric Biases in Availability and Attribution." *Journal of Personality and Social Psychology* 37 (3): 322–36. https://doi.org/10.1037/0022-3514.37.3.322.

Rothbaum, Barbara Olasov, Elizabeth A. Meadows, Patricia Resick, and David W. Foy. 2000. "Cognitive-Behavioral Therapy." In *Effective Treatments for PTSD: Practice Guidelines from the International Society for Traumatic Stress Studies*, 320–25. New York: Guilford Press.

Rothschild, Zachary K., and Lucas A. Keefer. 2017. "A Cleansing Fire: Moral Outrage Alleviates Guilt and Buffers Threats to One's Moral Identity." *Motivation and Emotion* 41 (2): 209–29. https://doi.org/10.1007/s11031-017-9601-2.

Russo, Richard. 1997. *Straight Man.* New York: Random House.

Ryan, Carey S., and Laura M. Bogart. 1997. "Development of New Group Members' in-Group and out-Group Stereotypes: Changes in Perceived Group Variability and Ethnocentrism." *Journal of Personality and Social Psychology* 73 (4): 719–32.

Ryan, Timothy J. 2017. "No Compromise: Political Consequences of Moralized Attitudes." *American Journal of Political Science* 61 (2): 409–23. https://doi.org/10.1111/ajps.12248.

Sawaoka, Takuya, and Benoît Monin. 2018. "The Paradox of Viral Outrage." *Psychological Science* 29 (10): 1665–78. https://doi.org/10.1177/0956797618780658.

Saxe, Leonard, Denise Dougherty, and Theodore Cross. 1985. "The Validity of Polygraph Testing: Scientific Analysis and Public Controversy." *American Psychologist* 40 (3): 355–66.

Schliesser, Eric. 2003. "The Obituary of a Vain Philosopher: Adam Smith's Reflections on Hume's Life." *Hume Studies* 29 (2): 327–62.

Schmidtz, David. 1994. "The Institution of Property." *Social Philosophy and Policy* 11 (2): 42–62. https://doi.org/10.1017/S0265052500004428.

Schmidtz, David. 2008. *Person, Polis, Planet: Essays in Applied Philosophy.* Oxford: Oxford University Press.

Schmitt, David P., and David M. Buss. 2001. "Human Mate Poaching: Tactics and Temptations for Infiltrating Existing Mateships." *Journal of Personality and Social Psychology* 80 (6): 894.

Schneller, Christian. 1867. *Märchen und Sagen aus Wälschtirol: Ein Beitrag zur deutschen Sagenkunde*. Innsbruck: Verlag der Wagner'schen Universitäts-Buchhandlung.

Sedikides, Constantine, and Mark D. Alicke. 2012. "Self-Enhancement and Self-Protection Motives." In *The Oxford Handbook of Human Motivation*, edited by Richard M. Ryan, 303–22. New York: Oxford University Press.

Sedikides, Constantine, Lowell Gaertner, and Yoshiyasu Toguchi. 2003. "Pancultural Self-Enhancement." *Journal of Personality and Social Psychology* 84 (1): 60–70.

Sedikides, Constantine, Lowell Gaertner, and Jack L. Vevea. 2005. "Pancultural Self-Enhancement Reloaded: A Meta-Analytic Reply to Heine (2005)." *Journal of Personality and Social Psychology* 89 (4): 539–51.

Sedikides, Constantine, Rosie Meek, Mark D. Alicke, and Sarah Taylor. 2014. "Behind Bars but above the Bar: Prisoners Consider Themselves More Prosocial Than Non-Prisoners." *British Journal of Social Psychology* 53 (2): 396–403. https://doi.org/10.1111/bjso.12060.

Simler, Kevin, and Robin Hanson. 2018. *The Elephant in the Brain: Hidden Motives in Everyday Life*. 1st ed. New York: Oxford University Press.

Simon, Herbert A. 1987. "Satisficing." In *The New Palgrave: A Dictionary of Economics*, edited by John Eatwell, Murray Milgate, and Peter Newman, 4:243–45. London: Macmillan.

Skitka, Linda J. 2010. "The Psychology of Moral Conviction." *Social and Personality Psychology Compass* 4 (4): 267–81. https://doi.org/10.1111/j.1751-9004.2010.00254.x.

Skitka, Linda J., Christopher W. Bauman, and Edward G. Sargis. 2005. "Moral Conviction: Another Contributor to Attitude Strength or Something More?" *Journal of Personality and Social Psychology* 88 (6): 895–917. https://doi.org/10.1037/0022-3514.88.6.895.

Skitka, Linda J., G. Scott Morgan, and Daniel C. Wisneski. 2015. "Political Orientation and Moral Conviction: A Conservative Advantage or an Equal Opportunity Motivator of Political Engagement?" In *Social Psychology and Politics*, edited by Joseph P. Forgas, Klaus Fiedler, and William D. Crano, 73–90. New York: Psychology Press.

Skitka, Linda J., and Daniel C. Wisneski. 2011. "Moral Conviction and Emotion." *Emotion Review* 3 (3): 328–30. https://doi.org/10.1177/1754073911402374.

Sloman, Steven, and Philip Fernbach. 2017. *The Knowledge Illusion: Why We Never Think Alone*. New York: Riverhead Books.

Smith, Adam. 1985. *The Theory of Moral Sentiments*. Indianapolis: Liberty Fund Inc.

Smith, Tom W., Kenneth A. Rasinski, and Marianna Toce. 2001. "America Rebounds: A National Study of Public Response to the September 11th Terrorist Attacks." *NORC Report*.

Solnit, Rebecca. 2015. *Men Explain Things to Me*. Chicago: Haymarket Books.

Somin, Ilya. 2013. *Democracy and Political Ignorance: Why Smaller Government Is Smarter*. 1st ed. Stanford, CA: Stanford University Press.

Steinmetz, Janina, Ovul Sezer, and Constantine Sedikides. 2017. "Impression Mismanagement: People as Inept Self-Presenters." *Social and Personality Psychology Compass* 11 (6): 1–15. https://doi.org/10.1111/spc3.12321.

Sunstein, Cass R. 2002. "The Law of Group Polarization." *Journal of Political Philosophy* 10 (2): 175–95. https://doi.org/10.1111/1467-9760.00148.

Sunstein, Cass R. 2009. *Going to Extremes: How Like Minds Unite and Divide.* Oxford: Oxford University Press.

Tappin, Ben M., and Ryan T. McKay. 2017. "The Illusion of Moral Superiority." *Social Psychological and Personality Science* 8 (6): 623–31. https://doi.org/10.1177/1948550616673878.

Tetlock, Philip E. 2002. "Social Functionalist Frameworks for Judgment and Choice: Intuitive Politicians, Theologians, and Prosecutors." *Psychological Review* 109 (3): 451–471.

Theriault, Sean M. 2008. *Party Polarization in Congress.* Cambridge, UK: Cambridge University Press.

Tosi, Justin. 2018. "Rethinking the Principle of Fair Play." *Pacific Philosophical Quarterly* 99 (4): 612–31. https://doi.org/10.1111/papq.12219.

Tosi, Justin, and Brandon Warmke. 2016. "Moral Grandstanding." *Philosophy and Public Affairs* 44 (3): 197–217.

Tuan Pham, Michel, Tom Meyvis, and Rongrong Zhou. 2001. "Beyond the Obvious: Chronic Vividness of Imagery and the Use of Information in Decision Making." *Organizational Behavior and Human Decision Processes* 84 (2): 226–53. https://doi.org/10.1006/obhd.2000.2924.

Vallier, Kevin. 2018. *Must Politics Be War?: Restoring Our Trust in the Open Society.* Oxford: Oxford University Press.

Vlahov, David, and Benjamin Junge. 1998. "The Role of Needle Exchange Programs in HIV Prevention." *Public Health Reports* 113 (Suppl 1): 75–80.

Vonasch, Andrew J., Tania Reynolds, Bo M. Winegard, and Roy F. Baumeister. 2018. "Death Before Dishonor: Incurring Costs to Protect Moral Reputation." *Social Psychological and Personality Science* 9 (5): 604–613. https://doi.org/10.1177/1948550617720271.

Vossen, Bas van der. 2015. "In Defense of the Ivory Tower: Why Philosophers Should Stay out of Politics." *Philosophical Psychology* 28 (7): 1045–63. https://doi.org/10.1080/09515089.2014.972353.

Vreese, Claes H. de. 2005. "The Spiral of Cynicism Reconsidered." *European Journal of Communication* 20 (3): 283–301. https://doi.org/10.1177/0267323105055259.

Vrij, Aldert. 2008. *Detecting Lies and Deceit: Pitfalls and Opportunities.* 2nd ed. Hoboken, NJ: Wiley-Interscience.

Walter, Nathan, and Sheila T. Murphy. 2018. "How to Unring the Bell: A Meta-Analytic Approach to Correction of Misinformation." *Communication Monographs* 85 (3): 423–441. https://doi.org/10.1080/03637751.2018.1467564.

Wellman, Christopher Heath. 2012. "The Rights Forfeiture Theory of Punishment." *Ethics* 122 (2): 371–393.

Wendt, Fabian. 2019. "In Defense of Unfair Compromises." *Philosophical Studies* 176 (11): 2855–2875.

White, Jonathan A., and S. Plous. 1995. "Self-Enhancement and Social Responsibility: On Caring More, but Doing Less, Than Others." *Journal of Applied Social Psychology* 25 (15): 1297–318. https://doi.org/10.1111/j.1559-1816.1995.tb02619.x.

Wilde, Oscar. 1903. *Lady Windermere's Fan: A Play about a Good Woman.* Paris: L. Smithers.

Will, George F. 2002. *With a Happy Eye, But . . . : America and the World, 1997–2002.* New York: Free Press.

Willer, Robb, Ko Kuwabara, and Michael W. Macy. 2009. "The False Enforcement of Unpopular Norms." *American Journal of Sociology* 115 (2): 451–90. https://doi.org/10.1086/599250.

Williams, Elanor F. 2007. "Naive Cynicism." In *Encyclopedia of Social Psychology,* edited by Roy F. Baumeister and Kathleen Vohs, 601–2. Thousand Oaks, CA: Sage. https://doi.org/10.4135/9781412956253.

Wittels, Harris. 2012. *Humblebrag: The Art of False Modesty.* New York: Grand Central Publishing.

Wodak, Alex, and Annie Cooney. 2004. *Effectiveness of Sterile Needle and Syringe Programming in Reducing HIV/AIDS among Injecting Drug Users.* Geneva: World Health Organization.

Yamamoto, Masahiro, and Matthew J. Kushin. 2014. "More Harm Than Good? Online Media Use and Political Disaffection Among College Students in the 2008 Election." *Journal of Computer-Mediated Communication* 19 (3): 430–45. https://doi.org/10.1111/jcc4.12046.

Zahavi, Amotz. 1975. "Mate Selection—A Selection for a Handicap." *Journal of Theoretical Biology* 53 (1): 205–14. https://doi.org/10.1016/0022-5193(75)90111-3.

Zahavi, Amotz, and Avishag Zahavi. 1999. *The Handicap Principle: A Missing Piece of Darwin's Puzzle.* New York: Oxford University Press.

Zell, Ethan, and Mark D. Alicke. 2011. "Age and the Better-Than-Average Effect." *Journal of Applied Social Psychology* 41 (5): 1175–88. https://doi.org/10.1111/j.1559-1816.2011.00752.x.

Zyl, Liezl van. 2018. *Virtue Ethics: A Contemporary Introduction.* New York: Routledge.

INDEX